Preservation and Technology

UNIVERSITY OF NORTHUMBRIA
AT NEWCASTLE LIBRARY
WITHDRAWN

National Preservation Office
Seminar Papers 3

Proceedings of a seminar
at York University

20–21 July 1988

Preservation and Technology

National Preservation Office
The British Library 1989

First Published 1989 by
National Preservation Office
The British Library
Great Russell Street
London WC1B 3DG

British Library Cataloguing in Publication Data

Preservation and technology: proceedings of a seminar
at York University, 20–21 July 1988. – (National
Preservation Office seminar papers; 3)
1. Libraries. Stock. Conservation
I. National Preservation Office II. Series
025.8'4

ISBN 0 7123 0172 0

Designed by Alan Bartram
Typeset by Bexhill Phototypesetters, Bexhill-on-Sea
Printed in England on British Library acid-free paper
by Henry Ling Ltd, Dorchester

Contents

Preface

After two highly successful seminars dealing with the problems of preservation from a chiefly intellectual point of view, it was felt that the third of these annual meetings should concentrate on possible practical solutions.

Progress in technology was chosen as a focus for discussion, and was perceived by the speakers as having both a positive and a negative side; the unproven and unpredictable nature of many new media will intensify the very problems of preservation for which they are heralded as providing a possible solution. The speakers emphasised the need for further research into the properties of the new media and caution in adopting any of them as the panacea for which we have been searching.

The sheer scale of the preservation problems in the abstract is so daunting as to make our efforts seem futile but the seminar provided a useful review of our achievements so far and encouraged us all to greater efforts.

List of contributors

Dr Peter Anderson	Scottish Record Office (Society of Archivists)
Christine Butler	Industrial Chemistry Group, University of Surrey
Dr Terry Cannon	Assistant Director, Research & Development Department, British Library
Dr David Clements	Director, Preservation Service, British Library
Henry J Heaney	Librarian and Keeper of the Hunterian Books & Manuscripts, University of Glasgow
Anthony J Loveday	Secretary, SCONUL
Professor A J Meadows	Head, Department of Library & Information Studies, University of Loughborough
Dr C A Millington	Department of Chemical Engineering, University of Surrey
Brenda E Moon	Librarian, University of Edinburgh
Ian R M Mowat	Librarian, University of Hull (Library Association)
Dr Cliff McKnight	HUSAT Research Centre, University of Loughborough
Jean M Plaister	Director, LASER
Mary Wilkinson	Head, Information Technology Unit, Public Record Office

A J Meadows

The medium and the message

Edmund Burke once commented that if a state could not adapt to change, neither could it succeed in conservation. He was thinking of the French Revolution, but his words are equally applicable to the present information technology revolution. One problem is that those people most concerned with the conservation of traditional materials are often those who have been least directly affected by information technology in the past. Judging by the current rate of development of information technology, this situation will not prevail for much longer. In fact, now may be the best time for formulating future policy with regard to the conservation of new materials. Archives of new media are beginning to accumulate, but have not yet – at least, outside government circles – become unmanageable. So this paper is aimed at discussing, in general terms, the factors that affect conservation policy for new media.

The variety of new media

The first essential is to recognise the great diversity of the media concerned. It is not just that data may be stored on magnetic tape, floppy discs, hard discs, etc. More importantly, each one of these storage media comes in a variety of forms. Suppose we consider magnetic tape, for many years the standard storage medium for digital data. Table 1 lists the main variants that have been in use over the past 30 years:[1]

The physical appearance of the tape has changed very little over this time: there is an agreed International Standard of a half-inch width, for example. But the arrangement of data on the tape – the number of tracks, the encoding of data, and the data density achieved – have all changed considerably. From the handling viewpoint, these differences can be as marked as the difference between books and microform.

Nor are these variations limited to digital data. Table 2 lists, for comparison, the different videotape formats that have been used over the past 30 years:

Table 1

Half-inch magnetic tape formats	*Current status*
7-track NRZI, 100 BPI	Obsolete
7-track NRZI, 200 BPI	Obsolete
7-track NRZI, 556 BPI	Obsolete
7-track NRZI, 800 BPI	Obsolete
9-track NRZI, 800 BPI	
9-track PE, 1,600 BPI	
9-track GCR, 6,250 BPI	
18-track RLL, 19,000 BPI	

NRZI = Non-Return to Zero Inhibit; PE = Phase Encoding;
GCR = Group Code Recording; RLL = Run Length Limited

Table 2

Videotape formats	*Current status*
2-inch quadruplex	Obsolete
2-inch quadruplex, double density	Obsolete
1-inch helical, type A	Obsolete
1-inch helical, type B	
1-inch helical, type C	
¾-inch helical, U-Matic	
½-inch helical, Betamax	
½-inch helical, VHS	
8 mm helical	
4 mm helical	

In this case, visual appearance has changed, as well as format.

Unfortunately, the position with regard to differences within a single medium is hardly improving. A glance at the diversifying uses of compact disc and videodisc (Table 3) can lead us to expect similar problems for these in the future.[2]

This plethora of forms raises not only questions concerning conservation, but also questions of access. Much more than for books, new technology must consider the merits of preservation *versus* conservation. Should the initial form be preserved, or should the contents be transferred to some standard medium? This is likely to be a key question in formulating a conservation policy for new media.

The medium/message relationship

At the most basic level, the answer is likely to depend on the relationship between the specific medium and the message it carries. Communication can

Table 3

Type of optical discs	*Types of data*	*Connected to*
Pre-Recorded		
CD-AUDIO (Compact Disc Audio)	Music	Hi-Fi
CD-ROM (CD-Read Only Memory)	Digital Data	Computer
CD-V (CD-Vision)	Music, Films	TV, Hi-Fi
CD-I (CD-Interactive)	Music, Digital Data, Images	TV, Hi-Fi, Computer
VIDEODISC	Films, Images, Music	TV-Hi-Fi, Computer
Recordable		
WORM (Write Once Read Many)	Digital Data	Computer
E/R-DOD (Erasable/Rewritable Digital Optical Disc)	Digital Data	Computer

be divided into two activities: the creation of a message and its reception. In the world of books, writing corresponds to creation and reading to reception. There is a little overlap in print media – in childrens' colouring books, for example – but the two activities are mostly separate. In many of the new media, creation and reception are much more closely linked, Magnetic tape, for example, is typically both written to and read from. The medium and the message, in this case, have an interactive element. This raises an interesting problem for the preservation of machine-readable information. Attempts by readers to deface or alter the contents of books are usually quite easy to detect. The same is not necessarily true of interactive media.

New technology involves new types of activity. Books deal with static images and text. Radio deals with sound. Television combines moving images with sound. Optical discs have the same coverage as television, plus text. Particular media are more appropriate for particular types of information. The zootrope and similar devices were a not very effective way of using book-type technology to produce moving images. Should poetry be read or heard? Up to the latter part of the seventeenth century the question hardly arose, since all reading was aloud. Now some poets are concerned with the layout of their words on a printed page, whereas others prefer channels that convey sound, as a recent debate about the dial-a-poem service has underlined. The most obvious indication that different media serve different purposes is, of course, the growth of 'tie-in' activities between media. Nowadays, for example, lists of best-selling books always include some which are TV tie-ins.

But it is not just that there are messages for media in much the same way that there are horses for courses. Similar information passed by different channels is received in different ways. It has been claimed, for example, that the amount of information remembered under test conditions depends on the channels used.[3] The tests suggest that typically we remember 10 per cent of what we read, 20 per cent of what we hear, 30 per cent of what we view and 50 per cent of what we hear and view simultaneously.

These differences between the various media lay down limits on what we can do to preserve contents by transfer to another medium. The question always is whether the original and the new medium are sufficiently closely related in their characteristics to make the transfer possible without losing important properties of the information transmitted. For example, digital data should normally be stored in machine-readable form, not as print out, since the former has properties, such as flexibility of retrieval, which the latter lacks. To some extent this balancing act is already under way. An increasing amount of information is published in parallel – hard copy plus machine-readable. The assumption behind such parallel publishing is that there are different markets for what is basically the same product conveyed via different channels.

Conservation of new media

Another fundamental question in deciding whether to transfer information from one medium to another is obviously the relative properties of the media in conservation terms. It may be necessary to transfer information to a new medium because the old medium is falling out of use and can no longer be read easily. But it makes much better sense to carry out transfers when the new medium has a longer lifetime than the original. For example, one of the arguments in favour of Computer Output Microfilm (COM) as a storage medium for digital data is that microfilm is a well-established medium with known archival properties. It should be added that a number of COM recorders are using dry-process film whose potential lifetime is still uncertain. (Standard microfilm has been based on wet-process film.) Yet the argument for microfilm in terms of storage lifetime is clearly a good one, in principle.

If we pursue the question of policy on new media further, the next stage is obviously to look at factors which limit their lifetime. The starting point is naturally with the physico-chemical properties of the media.

Properties of media

Hard copy can be divided into a substrate (paper) and a recording material (ink). The same holds true of other media, but the situation is generally complicated by the need for an additional substance to be deposited on the substrate. For example, magnetic tape consists of a plastic base, magnetic particles to act as the recording material and a binding substance to hold the base and the particles together. Unlike book paper, the substrate in new media usually has long-term stability: it is the material deposited on the substrate that presents problems. The plastic base of a magnetic tape has good stability. The binder is similar in its properties to the gelatin of photographic film. It will remain stable under the same conditions of temperature and humidity that microfilm requires. The most commonly used magnetic particles have been iron oxide, which has good chemical stability.

From the viewpoint of the parameters usually involved in conservation, magnetic tape therefore sounds quite a good bet. But new media involve new types of storage problem. Magnetic particles are necessarily affected by magnetic fields. Even if the storage place is not evidently affected by stray fields, the Earth's field is omnipresent. Again, though the tape is chemically stable, it is stored under tension and can stretch. When the tape is read, it spins at high speed. Rapid changes in tension can lead to pressure and friction, and so to the loss of data as the tape unwinds. Magnetic deterioration can be compensated for by 'refreshing' the data, in much the same way that road markings are repainted at intervals. Tension variations can be controlled by regular rewinding of the tape. Estimates of the frequency with which these activities have to be carried out vary with the importance of the data, but a generous figure would be every five years. This clearly rules out magnetic tape for archival storage, even though its chemical stability is good. As an example of the sort of effort involved, consider the following procedures used in a recent file storage experiment.[4]

Two copies of each file, an 'A' copy and a 'B' copy, are retained on magnetic tape, the 'A' copy in the installation's tape library and the 'B' copy in a remote tape library; both are re-copied every nine months. Each copy has its own serial number. A tape is acquired from an internal pool of tapes, the copy done and the original FRS (File Retention System) tape returned to the internal pool for later use. The copy system is used to 'refresh' the data regularly to prevent deterioration, as commonly required of all data stored on magnetic tape.

One difficulty is the continuing trend towards higher storage densities. The best way of achieving this has proved to be by using thin films of metal. Unfortunately, such films are often chemically unstable. This point is at the centre of a current debate on the storage properties of compact discs. In compact discs, the substrate is plastic impressed with surface pits by the master disc. The substrate is coated with metal to reflect laser light and then sealed with a layer of lacquer. The metal used most frequently is aluminium, which is fairly chemically reactive. In theory, the lacquer should isolate the aluminium from chemical reagents. It is currently claimed that, in practice, atmospheric moisture is not entirely excluded, so that the metal coating may oxidise in a short time, perhaps a few years. This sort of problem is not new. The first optical discs had a tellurium coating. They were withdrawn rapidly from the market when it was found that, because of oxidation, data stored on them only remained error-free for a matter of hours. Some current discs are being coated with gold, which is much less chemically reactive than aluminium. The drawback is the increased cost. In fact, the general lesson offered by compact discs seems to be that, if high density storage of archival quality is required, it may prove expensive to obtain.

One general query concerns estimating lifetimes for new media. The usual way is by speeding up the processes which are thought to be involved in the ageing of the medium. As part of the speeding up, these ageing factors are usually exaggerated. For example, compact discs may be exposed 30 times to the following cycle: (1) two hours at 65°C and 95 per cent humidity; (2) twelve hours at 40°C and 95 per cent humidity; (3) two hours at −30°C. It is always somewhat doubtful to what these conditions actually correspond in terms of lifetime in a controlled environment. From that viewpoint, compact discs stored archivally may survive longer than expected. But, equally, there may be ageing factors to take into account other than temperature and humidity. It has been alleged, for example, that the ink used in labelling compact discs can, in some cases, react with the lacquer and so lead to chemical changes in the disc. As with any medium, the only certain test is long-term assessment of deterioration but the urgency of the demand for a stable machine-readable mass storage device precludes taking this approach.

New conservation problems

The need to consider the storage problems caused by magnetic fields reflects the fact that new media may require additional restrictions on storage conditions over and above those required by older media. One example of this is the problem of dust. Magnetic tapes and discs, when they are in use, all run rapidly past reading heads. Small dust particles caught on their surfaces can lead to erasure of data during reading. Perhaps it is poetic justice that the particles most likely to cause this are of the size to be found in cigarette smoke: at least, it has provided a convenient excuse for many microcomputer crashes. This implies that a store for magnetic tapes and discs will require air filtration of a type not considered for book archives.

A problem common to many machine-readable storage devices concerns small-scale defects and their growth. For example, a close scrutiny of a typical compact disc will show that it possesses slight imperfections in the metal coating. The compact disc player, like other digital data readers, is designed to cope with gaps of this sort. It fills in the vacancy by extrapolating from the data on either side. In one sense this is a virtue since it means that some deterioration of the storage medium can be tolerated. The disadvantage is that by the time the defect has become large enough to produce a noticeable effect, some significant data may already have been lost. There is a contrast here with interactive media, such as magnetic tape. In these, an error correction process comes into action as the tape is played, so ensuring that deterioration can be corrected whenever the tape is read.

An indication of the overall consequences of deterioration is given by a study of archiving magnetic tape carried out in the United States in the early 1970s. It was found that 50 per cent of the tapes used and stored in the preceding ten years were no longer of acceptable quality and had to be discarded.[5] Although tape quality has certainly improved since then, the figures give some idea of the scale of the problem for new media as compared with the medium of print.

Software

The archival difficulties of machine-readable data lie as much in reading the data as in deterioration of the medium. In part this is a hardware problem – can the equipment handle the number of tracks on the magnetic tape, for example? But it is even more a software problem. In order to extract information, the operating system must be appropriate for the particular type of tape or disc in use. The difficulties this poses can best be illustrated by the example of UNIX, an operating system that has come to the fore during the past decade. It has already appeared in 30 versions, and no doubt more are to come. In addition, use of such systems relies on proper documentation. This is normally in hard copy, which is easy enough to store, but frequently goes missing from older systems, or was never properly collated in the first instance.

The need for experience

The most useful information on archival storage of new media obviously comes from those who are trying to do it. For example, the Knowledge Warehouse project, now under way, should provide some useful hints.[6] One of the earliest decisions in its management concerned the need to put some limits on what could be accepted and stored. The preferred standard is magnetic tape recorded on nine tracks at 1,600 bpi with the text prepared using a generic system of coding. Other media, such as discs, can be accepted subject to corresponding limitations. Despite this, a major activity of the Warehouse will be text conversion.

The data collected in the project so far give some feel for the archival problems currently posed by British electronic publishing. It has been found that somewhat over half of the works submitted by publishers during the trial period were prepared according to a generic coding scheme. This is mildly encouraging, but must be balanced against the output of other publishers who were apparently not entirely clear what they were doing. For example, some tapes labelled 1,600 bpi turned out to be 800 bpi. This highlights one of the drawbacks of electronic archiving, as compared with the archiving of books. Most defects or errors in print media can be noted by a quick visual scan; there is no such general equivalent for machine-readable media.

Preservation or conservation?

The difficulties of conserving new media might suggest that the best policy is to preserve information, whenever possible, on the better established media of paper or microform. This may be true in special cases, or as an interim measure, but there are clearly reasons for rejecting it as a general policy. One is the differing intrinsic properties of the media, mentioned earlier. Another is the storage space required. Though new media may impose more stringent conditions on storage facilities, the volume of space subject to these conditions is much smaller than for the equivalent amount of data on print or microform media. This mass storage factor is matched by a greater ease of handling: machine-readable data can be retrieved, copied and transmitted to readers much more readily than information recorded in traditional media.

Views regarding the future of archival storage therefore diverge considerably. On the one hand, it is suggested that information conveyed in printed form should be preserved for archival purposes in machine-readable form because of the latter's advantages. On the other hand, it is proposed that digital data intended for long-term retention should be stored on microform, rather than newer media, because of the latter's disadvantages. In either case, there will always be limits on how much data can be converted from one form to another; so preservation of this sort must follow some kind of selection process. It is by no means clear that agreement on what information should be transferred will be easy to reach. For example, the American Philological Association is working on a preservation programme for important printed materials in classical studies published between 1850 and 1918. As an experiment, five classical scholars were asked to decide which in a stack of relevant books should be preserved, and which not. The average voting on items was 3:2 – a slight change in the backgrounds of the participants would have altered the voting on a significant number of items.[8]

Conclusions

- Because different media have different properties, transfer between media is only possible in special cases. One urgent need is to determine when preservation by transfer is both feasible and desirable.

- Conservation of new materials with a relatively short lifetime is unavoidable. It is not clear what the most efficient methods of doing this might be. The practical experience of bodies involved in storage of machine-readable data is beginning to provide a guide. So is current research into the topic – for example, that supported by the British Library Research and Development Department. But the immediate need is for simple guidelines of the type already available nationally and internationally for print media and microform.

Notes

1. J C Mallinson *On the preservation of human and machine-readable records.* In: *Information technology and libraries* vol.7, no.1 March 1988.
2. *I'M* no.53 July-August 1988.
3. A H Thompson. *Knowledge acquisition and retention via different media.* In: *Audiovisual librarian* vol.12, no.4 1986.
4. *Data storage on optical disc – an experiment.* (IT series no.13) London: HMSO, 1986.
5. T Hendley. *The archival storage potential of microfilm, magnetic media and optical data discs.* Hatfield, Herts: NRCd, Hatfield Polytechnic, 1983.
6. M Buckingham. *The Knowledge Warehouse: technical issues.* In: *The electronic library* vol.6, no.1 February 1988.
7. C A Lynch and E B Brownrigg. *Conservation, preservation and digitization.* In: *College & research libraries* vol.47, no.4 July 1986.
8. R S Bagnall. *Involving scholars in preservation decisions: the case of the classicists.* In: *Humanities communication newsletter* no.10 1988.

Brenda E Moon and
Anthony J Loveday

Progress report on preservation in universities since the Ratcliffe Report

Abstract

The university and national libraries have long shown interest in aspects of preservation. Meetings of the Standing Conference in 1976 and 1981 gave detailed attention to the problems. Following the establishment of the National Preservation Office, SCONUL set up a Working Party to co-ordinate and stimulate activity in developing awareness and making provision for preservation of materials in member institutions. There has been an encouraging response as a result of heightened awareness.

This has been monitored and the results of a recent survey of fifty-three libraries using the same questions adopted for the Ratcliffe Report are reported in detail. The Report is used as a base line for comparison. Additional questions have been included to cover the preservation of non-book media. While there is still much to be done it is in this area that greatest effort is needed.

University and national libraries have long expressed interest in the problems of conservation and preservation although the available resources have not always equalled their concern. Furthermore, in the past a pre-occupation with older and rare material has taken precedence over the adoption of a conscious policy of selection and application of appropriate practices.

The records of meetings of the Standing Conference of National and University Libraries show that we devoted the Autumn meeting in 1976 to the theme of conservation. At this meeting Dr Seeley gave an overview of the problems associated with conservation and considered how best to meet the future needs of scholarship, while other British and Scandinavian colleagues contributed their thoughts on such matters as university library acquisition policy within a national context and the retention and relegation of library materials. There was little or no mention of types of library materials other than books and manuscripts, but a number of significant resolutions and recommendations were adopted at the final session which provided a continuing basis for preservation policies as valid today as it was twelve years ago.

Again, in 1980 the Conference used the six-monthly meeting at Loughborough to consider five contributions on various aspects of preservation policy and the need for guidelines. The meeting also attempted to repair the omission of non-book material from earlier considerations and looked in detail at the storage requirements of all types of material as well as emphasising again the need for some co-ordinated policy. In the course of this meeting it was announced that the project supported by the British Library Research and Development Department to establish the nature and state of preservation policies and conservation in British libraries was about to be launched. It was agreed however that detailed recommendations should await the outcome of the Ratcliffe Project funded by the British Library, which in due course culminated in the publication of the Ratcliffe Report[1] in 1984.

The most important progress however followed the establishment of the National Preservation Office, when SCONUL set up a Working Party to co-ordinate and stimulate activity in developing awareness and making provision for preservation of collections in member institutions. There has been an encouraging response as a result of this heightened awareness.

SCONUL has continued to draw attention to the need for action in the development of awareness of the problems and to promote sound preservation practice. For this purpose it established in 1984 its Working Party on Preservation, to promote strategies for the preservation of the intellectual content of material either through maintenance of the original form or by substitution policies. In the succeeding four years, it has arranged a seminar on the handling of materials for preservation for academic library staff, drawn up a statement on conservation, which has been adopted by the Conference, prepared a code on good preservation practices, produced a Disaster Control Checklist and recommended the use of bookbinding and repair procedures based upon the National Library of Scotland's manual of practice. It is currently working on the details of guidelines for the loan of materials for exhibition purposes. This has happened during a period of exceptional financial constraint during which all libraries have been enduring the most swingeing financial cuts in their resources of recent times.

Many were shocked by the findings reported by Dr Ratcliffe in his 1984 Report to the British Library and it is appropriate that we should at this time take stock of changes in the situation over the past four years. In preparation for this Seminar SCONUL reviewed the situation in its member institutions. Brenda Moon at Edinburgh University prepared a questionnaire based upon that used for the Cambridge Conservation Project designed to bring out the change which had taken place. It is on the results of this enquiry that this paper concentrates now, but it is appropriate that Miss Moon's contribution is acknowledged at this point in providing much of the data for this paper.

The questionnaire was distributed to the full membership (some 70 university and national libraries in the United Kingdom and the Republic of Ireland). Replies were received from fifty-three (a 76 per cent response rate). The following paragraphs summarise these replies, with notes on changes since the 1984 survey.

- Institutions having a preservation policy statement increased from two in 1982 to 17 at the present time; this does not include seven institutions which have policy statements in draft.
- 26 libraries had in-house binderies, employing an overall total of 259 bindery staff. This has increased to 27, but the number of bindery staff employed has dropped to 257. These figures do not include one institution with an in-house bindery managed by a commercial organisation. The British Library accounts for 100 of the staff reported.
- There were 15 conservation workshops employing 56 conservators, and this has changed to 20 workshops employing 74. Again 25 of these are accounted for by the British Library.
- 51 libraries had facilities for minor repairs; this has increased to 53. Against this, three libraries claimed to have no minor repair facilities, none of them having binderies or conservation workshops either.
- The number of libraries using outside craft binders has dropped from 33 to 32, and those using outside conservation facilities has dropped from 22 to 21. These figures exclude five libraries which reported that they used them rarely both in 1982 and in 1988. The figure of 21 institutions using outside conservation facilities excludes two libraries which reported using these facilities rarely in both years and one which used them only for pictures in 1988.
- The number of library Conservation Officers appointed has increased from 12 to 24.
- Air conditioning, which was limited to 15 institutions has only been extended by one; of these all except one are being maintained as was originally planned. In addition eight libraries in 1982 and nine in 1988 had partial air conditioning. However, the number of institutions monitoring the environmental conditions has increased from 25 to 36; in only 20 libraries were the environmental conditions appropriate for book preservation in 1982, although this has now increased to 23.
- In 1982 20 institutions reported that they systematically surveyed the state of books on the shelves and by 1988 this had increased to 29.
- Considerable improvement has been achieved in the training of library staff in good conservation practice: the 17 institutions undertaking this in 1982 had increased to 41 in 1988.

- In response to the question concerning access to scientific expertise for advice on conservation problems, 25 libraries reported in 1982 that they were able to obtain advice from within the parent institution and this has increased to 31; while 38 obtained such advice externally, with an increase to 49 currently.

- There has been an increase also in the number of libraries receiving conservation periodicals; this has gone up from 22 to 37. It is perhaps surprising that 100 per cent of libraries are not receiving such material in view of the very generous distribution arrangement for *Library conservation news*.

- The figures of the sums being spent each year on conservation show an increase from £7,270K to £7,715K. Of this £4,000K was spent in both years by the British Library. No other library spent over £500K in 1982, but two others did in 1988. In 1982 six other libraries spent between £100K and £500K, and this number increased to nine in 1988.

- 23 of our institutions reported that they are copying materials in stock either by microfilming or other means so that this material may be preserved by substitution. This represents an increase of three in the use of this method since 1982. A further five libraries reported occasional cases.

- There has been a considerable increase in the instruction and advice given to readers in the care and use of books and documents: 18 institutions provide this service compared with nine in 1982.

- While only two institutions reported to the Ratcliffe Survey that they had a disaster plan, some 19 libraries have now established them while a further ten report that they have disaster plans in draft form.

Because of the attention being given in this seminar to the preservation of new technologies we added to our questionnaire a number of additional questions about non-book media, which incorporate many of the technologies as well as adding to our knowledge of the situation about conventional non-book material.

When asked whether they had a preservation policy extending specifically to various media, a number of libraries reported that they did not hold all these items. Figures from institutions with such items in their collections were as follows:

microfilm: seven compared with five in 1982
microfiche: six compared with two in 1982
microprint: four compared with two in 1982

gramophone records: six compared with four in 1982
audiotapes: seven compared with three in 1982
compact discs: five compared with three in 1982

photographs: ten compared with seven in 1982
slides: six compared with four in 1982
videodiscs: three where formerly there were none
videotapes: six compared with two in 1982
CD-ROM: three currently have preservation policies

software: nine compared with two
magnetic tapes: seven where formerly there were none
discs: eight compared with one in 1982.

The situation over appropriate storage facilities for these various categories of material has been much more widespread:

microfilm: 40 compared with 39 in 1982
microfiche: 41 compared with 36 in 1982
microprint: unchanged since 1982 (29 institutions report having storage facilities)

gramophone records: 23 compared with 19 in 1982
audiotapes: 22 compared with 20 in 1982
compact discs: 17 compared with 14 in 1982

photographs: 24 compared with 19 in 1982
slides: 20 compared with 14 in 1982
videodiscs: 19 compared with 11 in 1982
videotapes: 20 compared with 11 in 1982
CD-ROM: nine compared with six in 1982

software: 19 compared with 11 in 1982
magnetic tapes: 16 compared with nine in 1982
discs: 18 compared with nine in 1982

CD-ROM for computer readable data: 14 compared with six in 1982.

In reply to a question on access to expertise for advice on preservation of these categories of material, the following responses were received:

microfilm: 36 compared with 30 in 1982
microfiche: 36 compared with 30 in 1982
microprint: 32 compared with 26 in 1982

gramophone records: 31 compared with 24 in 1982
audiotapes: 31 compared with 24 in 1982
compact discs: 28 compared with 20 in 1982

photographs: 32 compared with 26 in 1982
slides: 29 compared with 24 in 1982
videodiscs: 27 compared with 18 in 1982
videotapes: 25 compared with 19 in 1982
CD-ROM: 25 compared with 16 in 1982

software: 33 compared with 21
magnetic tapes: 30 compared with 19
discs: 30 compared with 19 in 1982
CD-ROM for computer readable data: 28 compared with 17 in 1982.

The problems of preservation of new media are two-fold: the preservation of material originally recorded in a new format (electronically or laser-produced) and the use of new formats for the purpose of substitution strategies.

It is clear that while libraries are starting to deal with some of the preservation problems in respect of the new technological products, and obtaining advice on the best methods of preserving this material, when the question of substitution methods arises they are still uncertain about the most durable means and the most economical medium. Only recently the statements made with great assurance about the permanence of CD-ROM have been challenged as corrosion of the plastic coatings and the disks themselves have, at the cheaper end of the market, become apparent. While microfilm has been established as reasonably permanent the task of transfer makes this an expensive process. Video and accoustic tapes we know have to be carefully protected against print-through and deterioration of image as well as needing suitable climatic storage conditions. No doubt weaknesses of the other media will gradually make themselves known. In the light of this uncertainty progress is likely to continue to be slow and it may well be that the use of permanent paper coupled with suitable climatic storage conditions will continue to provide the most economic long term answer to future preservation of the current print.

Finally to summarise the general impressions gained from the responses to the enquiry: there are encouraging signs of a growing awareness of the importance of preservation policy and practice in member libraries. Those librarians who had not been able to give much attention to the problems generally regretted it. Only one replied that he had more important things to think about!

Most librarians think of preservation in terms of books and manuscripts; few had specific policies with regard to non-book materials, though no doubt the habits which they had developed with regard to books and manuscripts will have heightened their awareness of the requirements for the preservation of other materials. (It is worth noting that the Public Record Office has developed an optical digital disk system for the preservation of magnetic materials.)

With the growing together of library and computing services in some universities the opportunities for librarians both to learn from and to teach their computing colleagues the factors to be considered in orderly storage of electronic and magnetic data are increasing.

The British Library has played a vital role in the noticeable improvements that have taken place in regard to book material, which our survey perhaps highlights. The 'Wolfson Grants' are undoubtedly an element in this and the work of the National Preservation Office has also been a major factor. Some work now needs to be done in stimulating awareness of the non-book preservation problems and in grappling with the very real problems that exist in the development of strategies for handling them. This seminar will undoubtedly draw greater attention to the problems and the importance of the preservation dimension of this growing volume of material.

Some years ago SCONUL and others endeavoured to stimulate interest in the archiving and storage of software and electronically generated data but a measure of either apathy or over-enthusiastic concentration on the novelty of the medium resulted in little progress being achieved.

Research is also needed into the cost benefits and technical characteristics of the new technologies for substitution policies and the results should be widely disseminated. Perhaps it would not be unreasonable to look to the National Preservation Office, in collaboration with other agencies, to give a lead in this difficult area.

Note

1. F W Ratcliffe and D Patterson, eds. *Preservation policies and conservation in British libraries: report of the Cambridge University Library Conservation Project.* London: British Library, 1984.

Peter D Anderson

Preservation, technology and the archivist

The invitation to the Society of Archivists to contribute to this seminar on preservation and technology, to discuss its members' current operations and their needs for long-term information storage, and especially to consider how technology might change the services which they provide and the implications this will have for preservation, has proved unexpectedly valuable. The fact is, that as far as can be ascertained, this is the first time the Society as such has been asked formally to address such a subject.

The forum for such discussion within the Society of Archivists is the Technical Committee. This committee has, over the past twenty years, achieved a very great deal, both in itself, through its offshoots the Conservation Group and the Conservation Training Committee, and by means of the Annual Instructional Meetings which it has organised. These meetings have provided an ever-expanding and lively focus for conservation and conservators. However, as these remarks may imply, the tendency has been for the committee to interpret its 'technical' remit as applying largely to conservation rather than other technical issues, or the broader matter of preservation. This is also true of the ICA. The problem is that there is a conservation aspect to practically all archival activities; those concerned with conservation issues have more than enough to occupy themselves, without exploring wider technical matters. Admittedly, the Technical Committee has rarely been asked for comment or assistance on matters outside conservation; but when so approached it has tended to rely on the particular expertise or knowledge of committee members or observers who happen to have other technical matters under their remit. At present these include the conservation officers of the National Library of Scotland and the Scottish Record Office, both of whom have responsibilities apart from that of conservation.

It would not be fair to say that archivists in general have not addressed technical questions. The ICA has had a microfilm committee for over twenty years; the Society of Archivists itself has had a computer applications committee since 1973; and Michael Roper, long a member of the Technical Committee, has made major contributions to the literature of both reprography and computerisation for archivists. It is simply that the present arrangement of the committees of the Society does not provide an arena for the discussion of the broad spectrum of technical matters. In the preparation of this paper therefore, numerous interested parties have been consulted including the assembled members of the Technical Committee itself.[1] If it helps to lay the foundation for a stated policy on the subject, well and good, but what is said today can be no more than the first few thoughts as far as the Society of Archivists is concerned.

Technical developments

There are perhaps four major areas in which technological developments can be said to affect archives and archivists at the present time: (1) conservation; (2) computerisation; (3) audio-visual technology; (4) photography and reprography. I propose to deal with the problems and benefits of each of these in turn.

Conservation

Developments in conservation are the only ones which are in fact, or at any rate in intention entirely beneficial from the archival point of view; that is to say they are dedicated solely to solving problems without in turn creating them. This does not mean that problems do not arise – changing documents by flattening them for example, can create difficulties of storage – but alone of the areas of technical development mentioned it has solely the welfare of the records at heart. All the others, while solving difficulties for other people, can create headaches for the archivist. Conservation has made tremendous technical advances, which require little rehearsal here. There have been developments in the treatment of acidity in papers, culminating in the possibility of using irradiation to strengthen paper structure; paper repair by leaf casting; freeze- and vacuum-drying; and the advances in paper and other chemistries which enable us to estimate the long-term effectiveness of new processes. When conservation does encounter difficulties, it is more often as a result of dispute within the conservation community, such as whether or not to laminate, the virtues or otherwise of soluble nylon, whether thymol is an effective fumigant or merely a salve to the conscience. But such problems arise from the best possible motive: relentless self-criticism regarding principles and practice.

Computerisation

Although it is true that the archive world (led by the Society of Archivists) preceded libraries in adopting a coordinated approach to conservation, the same cannot be said of its progress with computerisation. Library practice, where broad standardisation is possible, lends itself to computerisation, whereas attempts to standardise archival description in the light of computer developments do not in general seem to have arrived at any consensus. In the conservation unit, computers may be used primarily for administration, as in any other enterprise; at a time of energetic improvement of techniques, equipment and materials, they are especially valuable. From the archivist's point of view databases can render unnecessary the time consuming rearrangements often required by collections in the past. The collection can remain in its original organisation, or even disorganisation, while the computer provides chronological, numerical and categorical arrangements and searches on demand. Image capture, whereby a printed page can be copied electronically and converted into data for manipulation, though still in its infancy, is already making strides, and should in time solve the daunting problem of converting generations of archival cataloguing into machine readable form.

But the computer, for all the assistance it can offer to the archivist, is also a creator of problems – problems which are often beyond the archivist's control, and which may even now be building up to engulf him at some future date. Central to the problem of preservation is the spread of computerisation outside the record office; increasingly computers will come to provide archivists and record managers with the stuff they have to preserve, with all its consequent worries about archival quality, retrievability and compatibility in an age of fast-moving changes in technology, and questions of how best to accommodate the additions and amplifications of an ever-expanding database. Professor Meadows's remarks, particularly on compatibility and obsolescence, make one even more anxious about the future use of computers and management of their output.

Audio-visual technology

Audio-visual technology is the least rewarding of all from the preservation point of view in that, unlike computerisation or reprographic advances, it creates problems in one area without solving them in others. The products, audio or audio-visual, of oral history projects, reminiscence groups, local radio stations or freelance radio journalists, all offer the usual problems of tape preservation, but the techniques by which they are generated have no beneficial application, so far as I know, in preservation (except perhaps the general one of education). At national level, such material can be committed to the care of the British Library National Sound Archive, or, we hope eventually, the proposed Scottish Sound Archive. At local level, it is more difficult: transcribing and listing tapes is immensely time-consuming, as is the housekeeping involved; and conversion of tapes to disc, whether audio or video, is expensive. The lucky archivist will secure the services of an assistant specialising in audio-visual records, or make friends with an audio-visual librarian in the local library. A good Scottish example of this is the Orkney library where the archivist (on the library staff, but autonomous) has a part-time assistant whose primary function is that of sound archivist. She looks after a sound archive comprising a large private collection, tapes from BBC Radio Orkney, and modern project material, some of which she contributes herself.

Photography and reprography

Finally there is photography and reprography, and it is with this issue that I wish principally to deal today. I make no apology for this. Conservation developments are clearly of importance to archivists – in some cases vital to the records' very continued existence – but they are developments put at the disposal of the archivist by the conservator to solve old and recognised problems. To a great extent the archivist is in the hands of the conservator. Computer technology, as I hope I have indicated, is a very wide subject: it has its own forum within the Society of Archivists, and Mrs Wilkinson will make a much more valuable contribution on the subject than I ever could. Audio-visual records are a separate field and since they do not serve the archivist (as opposed to the historian), are best left to specialists.

This discussion therefore will examine the reprographic issues which most obviously concern archivists in ensuring adequate preservation of the records in their custody. Like computers, which both serve and make demands on the archivist, reprographic issues can be divided into two groups – problems and solutions.

The problems are twofold:

(i) how to satisfy the demand by readers for copies of records, electrostatic or photographic, with minimum damage;

(ii) how best to deal with change of format in continuing record classes (a particular concern of record managers), not only from the conservation and preservation standpoint, but also in terms of retrieval, reading and provision of copies. The solutions provided, particularly by microform, are: (1) to the problem of fragile originals, or of records in danger of becoming fragile through over-use:– the provision of microfilm substitutes, which can be studies and copied in place of those originals, (2) to the problem of space:– copies of material subsequently outhoused or destroyed, (3) to the problem of theft or accidental destruction of the records:– the provision of security copies.

From the researcher's point of view, copying is at the very least a great convenience and sometimes, as in the case of a scholar from abroad requiring a lengthy text, an absolute necessity. As a consequence readers can be quite insistent in their demands, and this can cause great difficulty; they may also complain about the cost of copying in archives, even when it is pointed out to them that cheap reader-operated machines are not appropriate for irreplaceable records and thus copying must be done by curatorial or qualified reprographic staff. In providing electrostatic copies, the archivist may seem to have an advantage over the librarian in that individual sheets of paper are much easier to copy than volumes; however manuscript volumes pose exactly the same problems as printed ones, and are often bigger than the maximum A4 size obtainable from the British Library pattern archival copier. (This machine can copy A3 sheets, but not as an 'archival' copier; it is this last point, among others, which caused the Scottish Record Office to decide not to purchase such a machine).

The new edition of BS5454, still making its way through the BSI system, sounds several notes of caution about electrostatic copiers. It recommends that parchments, volumes, documents in poor condition and documents too large for the top surface should not be copied. The physical problems caused by such copies – the flattening of volumes and tightly folded documents, the light-damage of repeated copying using a high-intensity scanner – are compounded by difficulties with the copiers themselves. Plans in particular should really not be copied in this way at all. The largest size of conventional electrostatic copier can handle A2-size material, but all such machines available at present have moving platens; such platens are discouraged by the British Standard, since they move the document about, and moreover the copier itself can be damaged by the strain placed on the motor driving the platen with a large volume of plans held down flat upon it. Other large electrostatic plan copiers require the original to be fed through them, clearly unacceptable for linen-backed manuscript plans, and impossible for large bound volumes.

The advantage of the electrostatic copier is that it deals in eye-readable paper copies, which remain a more attractive proposition to readers than any microform. Such paper copies are much cheaper than those produced by any other process. The disadvantages of it are several. Unlike any other reproductive process since the invention of moveable type, it uses no master: this means firstly that there is little decline in unit cost in the course of a long run (insofar as archivists ever indulge in long runs), and secondly that the original is subject to the intense light of an electronic scanner every time a copy is made. Neither of these problems is necessarily very serious; archivists do not often require long runs, and to avoid over-exposure of the original to light, an initial copy can be made from which to take further second-generation copies. There is a third problem however, and that is the electrostatic copier's relative lack of operational adaptability. It is this difficulty to which the archive world is particularly vulnerable.

Photocopier manufacturers usually follow a particular strategy in the design and marketing of their equipment. In some the emphasis is on reliability, or simplicity of operation. These qualities are clearly to be welcomed; but others, such as speed or the number of sophisticated features – document feeds, the facility to copy two pages on separate A4 sheets on a single pass, the collating or stacking of copies, the elimination of black edges to the paper, the editing out of particular parts of the image – are often of little practical use to the archivist, who is involved in producing single copies of a wide variety of paper objects of different sizes, from the platen. And the resources are rarely available for any one institution to develop a machine to its own specifications. About four years ago the Scottish Record Office investigated the possibility of developing a photocopier capable, as some early Xerox machines had been, of reversing the image from a paper negative; it came to nothing, but the figure of £80,000 was mentioned in development costs.

If you consider just what an ideal archival copier might be like, (and by that I mean archival, as opposed to library) it becomes a sophisticated and expensive machine. It should include the book cradle of the existing archival copier, but should be capable of handling paper sizes from A5 to at least A3; it should be possible to switch easily from cradle copying to platen copying and back again without undue loss of quality; the platen, and the glass masking the scanner over the cradle should protect the item from ultra-violet light; the paper tray should be capable of taking foolscap paper, travelling both sideways and lengthways along the paper path. (It would also suit the Scottish Record Office if it could reverse the polarity of the image, while taking no more time from one button-push to another than a conventional machine, but as the Office's demands are to some extent eccentric, it would be unfair to insist on these.)

It is clear from this that a switch to microform, employing film or fiche for volumes and aperture cards for plans, has much to recommend it. Microform is a much more adaptable medium, and as reader-printers increase in sophistication, it is quite possible to obtain plain paper copies from microform in just about any size up to A0. A master copy should be made of any records which are at all likely to be copied repeatedly; further copies can then be made without recourse to the original.

When we come to the question of change of format, there are perhaps three chief areas in which an archivist may encounter problems. Firstly there are formats left over from the past. By this I do not mean paper and parchment; the capacity for parchment and traditional paper to last indefinitely if properly cared for has been established over centuries. What is meant is earlier reprographic formats. The Scottish Record Office and Buckinghamshire County Record Office both have in their possession photostat negatives. Reproducing these has proved difficult for Buckinghamshire, and the SRO has offered help in copying them photographically. The SRO's own problem has proved a nightmare. It is on a much larger scale, consisting of 30,000 bound volumes each containing 250 bound negatives, a total of 7.5 million images. The Photostat process itself is obsolete, but neither it nor any of its modern successors would be capable of the cheapness or speed of turnover achieved by the electrostatic copier. Nothing other than the electrostatic process can cope with a demand for copies which runs at between 1.25 and 1.5m copies of different kinds per annum (perhaps a quarter of these being from photostats). The SRO's solution to the problem highlights the difficulties of dovetailing available technology, sophisticated though it may be, to unusual problems. It consists of a mixture of technologies: conventional copiers (copying 'the hard way', with a 96 per cent toner coverage of the paper, as opposed to the conventional four per cent – this originally proved impossible for many machines and injurious to others, but advances in technology seem to have improved performance); laser copiers (capable of reversing the image and only prevented from being the complete answer by their slowness of operation); and photographic copiers, still used for copies larger than A3 or for very poor quality originals.

Secondly there is the format of the future: machine-readable records. Indeed, this is still largely in the future, but its likely consequences are imminent and far-reaching. In the medium term the optical disk promises to provide archivally permanent and easily searched means of storing electronic data; no doubt record managers are watching carefully the Public Record Office's work in this field. In the longer term, its capacity to store images may prove of value in superseding microfilm, with its seemingly finite lifespan, with something of greater archival permanence. One's feelings about this prospect may be mixed. On the one hand improvement in the archival quality of modern records is always welcome; on the other hand who knows what headaches it may create in the future? Even the possible permanence may be an illusion; the manufacturers of the optical disks used by the PRO guarantee their disks for 30 years, but not the data upon them. Experiments are being conducted to see how the plastic disk coating, or the metal beneath are affected by time, oxidation or adverse climatic conditions.

At present the most significant change in format that the archivist is likely to meet remains the switch to microform. The biggest problems with this are archival quality, retrievability and readability. I myself inherited the headache of a collection of electrostatically printed microfiche (not created by the Scottish Record Office!) where the image, far from being archivally permanent, could actually be erased by gentle rubbing. So poor were they that when they were transferred to silver halide stock, the originals were not used for copying; their diazo duplicates being employed instead. Other difficulties have included records on 16mm microfilm cartridges of obsolescent design run on ageing equipment (solved by jacketing the film), and roll film court process indexes, an annual series which had already been in existence for five years before it was accessioned and found to be altogether unsuitable (a solution is still under discussion). It is important that transmitted or inherited microforms should be examined carefully, and that any organisation whose records are likely to find their way into an archivist's care should be persuaded at the outset to select a suitable medium of microfilm conforming to the appropriate British Standards. Retrievability and organisation are a constant headache with microforms. The linear nature of roll film makes it hard to skip, particularly without the use of a powered microfilm reader, and badly organised miscellaneous film is difficult to use. 'Blipped' film is clearly an advantage, but readers capable of tackling blips are expensive, reader/printers even more so.

So much for the problems; what is the best way of using the advantages of microform in archives? The ideal situation from the archival and conservation viewpoint envisages microfilm copying of everything in the archive, preserved in the form of silver halide negatives, sited in a different building from the originals, with diazo duplicates made available in the search room, the original records being viewed only under special circumstances. At present the most likely format for such film would be 35mm roll microfilm, though there is a school of thought which seems to suggest that this may yet be superseded by 16mm roll, as film quality and resolution improves; certainly such a development would mean a considerable saving in money. In such an arrangement there may also be a place for microfiche, jacketed film and aperture cards.

In circumstances where all or a large proportion of an archive's holdings are available on microform, the clear possibility arises of self-service ordering, reading and copying. Such arrangements are already commonplace in non-archival institutions such as the Scottish Companies Office (using jacketed film), and some material is available for perusal on the open shelves in the

Public Record Office and some English local authority record offices. Unfortunately the transfer of an archive's entire holdings to microfilm remains a mirage; in a small record office because of the expense involved, in a large institution due to a combination of expense and sheer scale. The Scottish Record Office examined the possibility of transferring the modern (1869 onwards) Register of Sasines, the central register of conveyances in Scotland, on to microfiche, since it is under constant siege by legal clients. It was estimated that such a task would take 150 person/years to complete and cost, at a conservative estimate, £2.5m; and this was to say nothing of other practical issues such as quality control.

Archives therefore have to set themselves strictly limited objectives. Programmes of microfilming for the archivist's own purposes are difficult to justify to auditors and unglamorous to disinterested sponsors. The Public Record Office's experience seems to be that conservation filming fights a constant war with reader-generated filming, and the largest filming project in Scotland – that of filming Scottish newspapers (admittedly a library rather than an archival project) – has found it extremely difficult to attract funds. The common policy therefore is to use requests from readers as justification for microfilming particular groups of records. The researcher is charged for a duplicate where an original exists, but where it does not then he or she is charged for both original and duplicate, though receiving only the latter. The problem with relying too heavily on such a method is that the results are haphazard and dependent on research interests which may be unique to individuals. Neither the film, nor the records on which it is based, may ever be asked for again.

There is one way in which readers and archivists can come together with profit. I said earlier that it seems difficult to attract disinterested sponsors to filming projects. It is quite different with *interested* sponsors, who may well have their own large-scale copying agencies. The best known of these is the church of Jesus Christ of Latter-day Saints, the Mormons. They have filmed on a large scale for many years, either by paying for institutions to film large classes of records in their entirety (the Free Kirk session records is a Scottish example currently under way); or by themselves filming on the premises, as they have done in the General Register Office for Scotland and elsewhere, providing microfilm for the institutions themselves by way of payment. But the Mormons are not the only people to pursue this line; the India Office Library and Records estimates that 40 per cent of their microfilm output is produced on 'sponsored' cameras, sponsored in particular by the Gulf States, who are interested in material relating to their part of the old India trade route. Clearly such an arrangement can be of inestimable value but it is unfortunately of limited application. It is the experience of the Scottish Record Office that other institutions which film on a large scale tend to request artificial assemblages of material relating to their areas of interest which are useful for little else and are indeed one of the biggest bugbears of any archive service, mopping up flagging, filming and checking time, with little to show for it beyond (one hopes) a single satisfied customer.

I hope that this paper has not laid too great stress on the problems and headaches with which modern technology confronts the archivist. The attempt has been to look at both sides of the question positively – to see the advantages offered by scientific developments on the one hand, and to look sensibly at how to prepare for change, even when it is impossible to predict just what sort of change it will be. At present the Civil Service College offers a course entitled *Managing technological change,* and this I think describes aptly a large proportion of the archivist's job in the future. It may not mean quite what the Civil Service College has in mind – not so much harnessing technology as accommodating the results of developments elsewhere – but perhaps for that very reason it provides an exciting, if exhausting prospect. For the future we confront a world in which opportunities for proliferation are effortless and unlimited: we will make copies on personal machines little bigger than the papers they produce; the originals will be on paper, on microform, on videodiscs; we will send facsimiles to the other side of the world in seconds, in any format we choose. What then will be the role of an institution dedicated to the preservation of unique originals? To reverse McLuhan (and Professor Meadows), the message will be important, not the medium: the latter, unlike the palimpsest of old, will tell us little, being nothing more than a vehicle for the data, the message. How librarians view this prospect I do not know, but it may be that the very distinction between archives and libraries will break down, and such institutions as we know them become only museums of obsolete media.

Note

In the compilation of this paper I am particularly grateful to the following: Michael Roper, David Thomas, Tim Padfield and their colleagues of the Public Record Office; Helen Forde (also of the PRO) and John McIntyre of the National Library of Scotland, chairperson, and secretary respectively of the Society of Archivists Technical Committee; Penelope Tuson and Andrew Cook of the India Office Library and Records; Anna Sheldon of the British Library; and Andrew Broom of the Scottish Record Office, secretary of the ICA committee on conservation and restoration. They should not, however, be held in any way responsible for the views expressed here.

Ian R M Mowat

The role of the Library Association

The presence here this afternoon of an ordinary member to speak on behalf of the Library Association illustrates both the strength and the weakness of our leading professional body. The Library Association headquarters staff are an excellent group of hard working professionals but the very breadth of the area they are expected to cover makes it difficult for them to contribute as experts in any particular specialism. In theory, expertise is provided from the membership but when the number of ordinary members with available expertise is also limited, as it is in preservation, and when that number is further reduced because the leading figures are either not available or are present today in some other capacity, the Association's reserve quickly descends to a level where expertise is most notable by its absence. It should be made clear also that any views expressed are entirely personal and do not necessarily represent the official line of the Association's policy-making bodies.

In the preparation of this paper a considerable debt of gratitude is owed to Anne Hobart, the Library and Information Services Secretary of the Library Association, for the investigatory work she has done.

Historical background

The Library Association has a long and honourable role in the preservation of library materials. As long ago as 1905 a Book Production Committee was created with Ernest Savage, later to gain renown as the innovative librarian of Edinburgh City Libraries, as Honorary Secretary.[1] It took until 1913 for the Library Association's leisurely procedures to publish an 'interim report'. Perhaps because of the outbreak of the First World War no final report was forthcoming. However, the work of the Committee had already borne some fruit since Cambridge University Press approached it for a binding specification for the great eleventh edition of the *Encyclopaedia Britannica* of 1910/11 and the Committee is credited with the introduction of the standard library binding.

It seems to have taken the Library Association some time to recover its interest in conservation in the post-war years. Not until 1928, indeed, was a Committee on the Durability of Paper set up, being charged with the responsibility of completing the interim report of its pre-war predecessor. This committee included amongst its membership another of the great names of British librarianship, Arundel Esdaile of the British Museum. In its turn the Committee produced *Book construction* in 1931.[2]

This task completed, the Library Association appears to have sat back on its laurels. Another world war intervened before further activity ensued and even in the aftermath of war it took some time for interest to awaken again. Almost inevitably the post-war expansion of libraries and the growth of information turned the attention of many librarians to newer problems: automation, new buildings, pro-active rather than re-active services and the like. Demands upon library managers' time grew ever more pressing and in the competition for attention the more stable and established activities seemed relatively less important. Cause and effect are difficult to disentangle but it is evident that the contributors to failure feed on each other. When a subject ceases to be accorded top priority it loses the attention of the leading figures, it begins to seem old-fashioned and non-productive in career development terms and suddenly no-one wants to know – even when age old problems continue more or less unabated.

So it was with preservation and its associated topics, historical bibliography and the history of book production. In the early era of post-war library school expansion those traditional topics were high on the agenda and it is perhaps no coincidence that the principal evidence of Library Association involvement in conservation at this time should have been the publication by the Association of Assistant Librarians of Clough's *Bookbinding for librarians* in 1957 as a textbook for students.[3] But by the late 1960s the old staples were beginning to be dropped from the curriculum and in the seventies and early eighties they all but disappeared from library schools. A whole new generation of librarians has grown up, largely ignorant of preservation.

The Library Association is a collection of about 25,000 individuals. At its best it can rise above individual weaknesses to exercise an influence for good on the development of the profession but, as an Association, it has to reflect the current interests and concerns of the membership. As interest moved away from the curatorial aspects of librarianship it was hardly surprising that the Library Association should weaken its involvement in this area of activity.

Despite this, in the latter part of 1970 the Research and Development Committee of the Library Association set up a small working party on the conservation of library materials, to consider what effective steps might be taken to make and keep librarians aware of the problems of physical deterioration and of the methods available for treatment and preservation. As before, the working party included amongst its members some of the leading luminaries of the profession, with Dr K W Humphreys of Birmingham University as the chairman and, once again, the product was a pamphlet, *The care of books and documents* which was published in 1972.[4] This very practical little document, giving guidance on specific treatments and sources of supply has stood the test of time and remains a most useful guide, despite the inevitable dating of some of the contents.

As after earlier bursts of activity, so on this occasion the successful completion of a specific project seems to have diminished official interest in the problems of conservation and preservation, and for a lengthy period the Association's attention was turned, in keeping with the interests of the majority of its members, to other pressing matters. Indeed, in January 1972 the working party was wound up and an 'Advisory Panel was constituted to be available for consultation by correspondence'.[5] Whatever correspondence there may have been seems to have been kept a fairly closely guarded secret.

However, the more traditional teaching of the subject declined just at a time when there was growing support for conservation in a much wider sense. The continuing fringe efforts of Greenpeace and the Ecology Party have been but the more extreme manifestations of a general movement which has seen the membership of the National Trust, for example, grow from 165,000 in 1968 to 1,200,000 in 1988.[6] Regrettably, the Library Association, instead of being in the vanguard of this movement, was initially somewhat tardy to mirror national developments in its own concerns; but a combination of the trend of history and the stark realities of old problems made more pressing by new conditions eventually resulted in the Association once more entering the fray in a formal capacity.

This re-entry led to the creation of a new Sub-committee on Conservation (later re-named to include Preservation) but the formal creation was, in part at least, a response to an already existing interest among some elements of the Association's membership.

The University, College & Research Section, for example, as the Library Association group with perhaps the most widespread concern for conservation matters, was already looking at the matter. The Group's Annual Study Conference in 1982, which addressed itself, amongst other things, to the issue of conservation, was planned and held before the Sub-committee got off the ground and was itself a response to subterranean stirrings within the depths of the membership.[7]

The Sub-committee on Preservation and Conservation – aims and achievements

Officially, the Sub-committee came into being as a result of a paper presented by Russell Bowden, the present Deputy Secretary-General, to the Professional Development and Education Committee in January 1981, pointing out that there was a growing concern, both nationally and internationally, about the conservation problems not only of books and other documents but also of newer media forms. He drew attention to the activities of IFLA and SCONUL in this area and recommended the creation of a small sub-committee on conservation.[8]

After the usual lengthy gestation period the Sub-committee eventually met for the first time in May 1982 and has since convened on a further fourteen occasions, until the end of last year. It is, perhaps, a sign that this phase of the Association's involvement in preservation may be coming to an end that the Sub-committee has not met this year for lack of business! Whatever the future may hold, however, I think the present Sub-committee may be reasonably content with their endeavours and achievements to date compared with the output of the preceding committees. As in the past, the Association has not lacked for big names to be involved – on this occasion, for example, Dr Fred Ratcliffe, a founding member and present Chairman of the Sub-committee. The Sub-committee has been particularly fortunate to have access to some of the most prominent preservation experts in the British book world, such as Nicolas Barker, while Barry Bloomfield, who served as Chairman for most of its life to date, must be held primarily responsible for such achievements as can be credited to the group.

At its first meeting the new Sub-committee agreed that the prime objective of the Library Association 'must be to awaken the profession to the problems and the need to resolve them'. Dr Ratcliffe also pointed out that although those associated with the recently established British Library Research & Development Department research project (which was to lead in 1984 to the Ratcliffe report[9]) could be trusted to understand the significance of conservation, there was lacking a central framework within which individual libraries could operate. He identified other problems as being concerned with the absence of conservators, or even a structure for them to fit in to in most libraries and the lack of coordination between custodians, administrators, technicians and scientists.[10]

If it all sounds too familiar it should be appreciated just how much progress has been made in the last few years. The state of road construction in the Highlands of Scotland, if hardly a model at present, is certainly a great advance upon the roadless desert of the early eighteenth century. The man to whom much of the credit for the beginnings of this improvement is usually attributed is General George Wade of whom it was written:

> Had you seen these roads before they were made,
> You would lift up your hands and bless General Wade.[11]

It might be no exaggeration to see Dr Ratcliffe in the role of some latter day General Wade to whom all should, in their different ways, give blessing! It may be that most of these blessings are directed to him in his role as Director of the BLR&DD project and subsequently for his work at the National Preservation Office but his contribution to the work of the Library Association has also been considerable.

The Sub-committee further agreed at its first meeting that its objectives should include: the monitoring and evaluation of conservation needs at national and local level to ensure that they received consideration in the debate on national information policies; the obtaining of resources for conservation;

the promotion of educational opportunities; the improvement of the position of conservators in libraries.

The remainder of this paper reviews the success or failure of the Library Association in achieving these aims to date. It is to be hoped that the review will be taken only as a progress report, rather than an obituary, as there are clearly many areas in which there is still much to do. Above all, in the area which is the keynote theme for this conference, that of new technology, the Library Association has not been noticeably conspicuous for its successes, or even for its involvement.

The reasons for this are fairly obvious. Although attention to the needs of the new media was determined to be a priority area for the Sub-committee at an early stage, it has rarely figured in the discussions which have taken place and even less often has there been an actual initiative. Because the Library Association, naturally enough, has done its best to select for membership of the Sub-committee those with an interest in, or knowledge of conservation or preservation, it has almost by definition excluded those whose primary concern is with new technology. That is not to say that individual members of the Sub-committee have not been willing to pay some attention to the challenges of preserving the output of new technology. Early membership did, in fact, include a representative of the Audio-Visual Group, who played a significant part in initiatives in that direction.[12] The more senior members of the Sub-committee need to be acquainted with new technology as part of their working lives, whatever their preferences, and the generalists who sit on the Sub-committee by reason of representing relevant groups of users rather than because of subject expertise, may actually be as interested in new technology as preservation.

However, generalists frequently have no expertise in any area, while specialists in one discipline can rarely spare the time or the energy to be equally knowledgeable in another. It would be true to say, therefore, that few, if any, on the Sub-committee would feel able to pronounce on the problems of new technology with quite the same authority as on the options in bookbinding, paper conservation or environmental control. It might, indeed, be argued that the existing Sub-committee membership should be reorganised in the near future to take account of the need for a change of direction. This would not only revitalise the energies of the group but also provide expertise capable of tackling these outstanding problems.

It would be incorrect, nevertheless, to give the impression that the Library Association has shirked its responsibilities in the case of new technology. The strength of the Association lies in its abilities to coordinate the specialist activities of various groups. If the Sub-committee on Conservation and Preservation has not yet felt able to tackle some of the outstanding problems in depth, there are other sections within the Library Assocation where complementary expertise exists.

The University College & Research Section, as has been indicated, has already taken independent initiatives and it is possible to see, in the near future, that new technology itself holds at least some of the answers to some of the problems which it poses. As part of its general plan to introduce an information system the Library Association proposes to create an index of expertise. A prototype, confined to experts in information technology itself, has already been created by the Information Technology Group, but the future prospect of an electronically accessible index on which the Library Association can call to provide suitable membership of committees and to help with specific issues as they arise holds out the hope that a major improvement in the quality of advice available both inside and outside the Association is near at hand. This will only be achieved, of course, if the will, and the finance, to carry the project through are at hand and if sufficient care is taken in the preparation of the index to make it easy and reliable to use.

The index may become increasingly valuable if the present intention of broadening the base of the Library Association to include a larger proportion of those in the sunrise areas of the information industry proves successful. An index containing details of both traditional conservators and experts in current technology could be a useful tool in bringing together overlapping interests which at present tend to operate in different milieux.

For the present, it is perhaps natural that the Sub-committee has been unable to achieve a uniform success in all the objectives it set itself. There are considerable limitations on the Association's ability to direct resources. It is no longer, if it ever was, the central focus of chief librarians and in an era of government devoted to reducing public expenditure such limited lobbying power as previously existed has been further reduced. If the Library Association no longer claims primacy in coordinating the decisions of chief librarians, no more does it maintain a monopolistic oversight for the profession as a whole. The later twentieth century proliferation of expert bodies and sub-bodies is as apparent with respect to conservation and preservation as it is in other areas and, possibly in contrast with the political climate which prevailed when the previous Library Association committees came into being, the existence and activity of alternative bodies is an important factor in the current phase of development.

So far as conservation and preservation are concerned the existence of more than one directing force has probably been beneficial, in part because of the considerable overlap of membership between existing bodies. The same names, those of Barry Bloomfield, Fred Ratcliffe and David Clements for example, occur in multiple contexts; one minute with a Sconul hat, another as a Library Association representative, while yet again with the imprimatur of the British Library. A partial exception to this clubbable cooperation may be seen in the attitude of the Departments of Library and Information Studies/Science. The abandonment by the Library Association of its previously dominant role in basic professional education and the recent suspicion that some, at least, of the old 'library schools' are attempting to distance themselves from their traditional market place has meant that the links between the professional body and the educators have not been quite as strong as might be wished. Even there, however, the presence of Professor John Feather on the Sub-committee has provided a link between the Association and the library schools and there is some evidence that a total abandonment of relevant teaching has been avoided.

A critic might question the recurrence of the same people in different guises, but to someone operating on the edge of all this activity the system does seem to have had the advantage of leading to organisational specialisation. The Library Association Sub-committee has, over the past few years, steadily narrowed its primary field of activity. While continuing to pay lip service to the place of conservators and to the need for more resources, the greatest effort in the immediate past has gone into those areas where the Library Association can make its strongest contribution. The Association has been more than willing to give such support as it can to the efforts of, for example, the National Preservation Office; but it has not attempted to compete with the National Preservation Office where the expertise of the latter could be effectively deployed.

Thus, for some time, the Sub-committee considered following the example of its predecessors in publishing a volume of guidance. It was felt, however, that the productions of the National Preservation Office would be a more authoritative vehicle for conveying the necessary information and the Sub-committee has preferred to concentrate its attention on facilitating the work of others, on its initial prime objective of awakening the profession to the problems and the need to resolve them, and on the follow-up requirement in developing an educational base and in lobbying where it could have some hope of making an impact.[13]

When new terms of reference were drawn up in April 1986, their broad resemblance to the original terms masked a significant increase in the importance of the educational and promotional aspects of the Sub-committee's work. This change of emphasis, 'recognising the difficulty in progressing work when resources are limited',[14] became explicit in a further review in March 1987 when it was agreed to concentrate on education and training.[15]

Education has taken two forms: the general effort to awaken the membership at large to the problems; and more specific targetting of those with a conservation or preservation role. Despite the Sub-committee's avoidance of the traditional report or pamphlet, it has almost certainly been responsible, even if only indirectly, for the publication of more preservation-related literature than any previous committee. The effort has been most particularly concentrated upon the publications of the Association itself and constant persuasion and encouragement from the Sub-committee has resulted in a regular flow of articles and news items related to preservation appearing in the *Library Association record* over the past three or four years, amounting to more than at any time certainly in the last twenty years. Cynicism suggests that publication alone may not do much to alert librarians to matters of importance, but quantity has some impact and the efforts of the Sub-committee have been helped by the transformation of the *Record* itself. Under its current editor it appears that an increasing proportion of the membership have actually taken to reading the journal which appears before them once a month.

In any event, with the encouragement of the Sub-committee articles and notices have appeared in the *Record* on such varied topics as: permanent paper, a core curriculum for the teaching of conservation, a survey of library school attitudes, and the continuing activities of the Sub-committee itself.[16] It should not be forgotten that achieving a high profile is not necessarily an easy task. To obtain space, even within the main professional journal, requires a fair degree of persistence and the successes conceal a substantial number of failed attempts to increase the coverage of conservation and preservation matters.

If the *Library Association record* has served to keep the membership at large abreast of developments and proposals, the other publications of the Library Association have also been used to get a more specific message across. The *Journal of librarianship* in 1985 carried a number of papers delivered at a 1984 seminar on education for conservation, organised by the Library Association and aimed primarily at the library schools.[17]

While the printed papers of this seminar represented a substantial contribution to current thinking, the highlight of the Library Association's publication effort to date must be the proceedings of the 1986 Annual Conference at Harrogate: *Preserving the word*.[18] Effective lobbying by members of the Sub-committee and a recognition by the conference organising committee, encouraged by Alex Wilson, of the timeliness of the topic, achieved a coup in having the whole of the 1986 conference devoted to preservation and conservation. The publication of the proceedings has enabled the message to reach an audience far wider than that of the conference itself.

The Sub-committee has also successfully drawn to the attention of the Association's membership a number of existing publications. The IFLA *Guidelines*[19] and the National Preservation Office's *Survival kits,*[20] for example have been extensively distributed at conferences and through circulation with the *Library Association record.*

Changes within Library Association practices clearly have been a target for the Sub-committee's attention. After effective lobbying by Barry Bloomfield, the Library Association's Grants and Awards Sub-committee agreed in 1986 that it would include in its letters of invitation for the submission of books for prizes, and also in the terms of reference for judges, a form of words which would encourage publishers and judges to look for the use of acid-free paper in the works submitted. Library Association Publishing Limited, though like all publishers expressing concern at the commercial consequences of too rapid and overwhelming a transfer to permanent paper, has at least taken heed of the Sub-committee's promptings, and it was encouraging for the Sub-committee to discover that prior to its own advances the *Library Association record* had already gone over to the use of acid-free paper.[21]

It may be true that many librarians remain sceptical or antagonistic to the greater prominence being accorded to preservation but there can be no doubt that greater prominence has been achieved and that the efforts of the Sub-committee have been instrumental in this achievement. The almost exasperated acknowledgement by the Sub-committee parent, the Library and Information Services Committee, of its energetic approach and the occasional *frisson* caused by the Sub-committee's willingness to trespass in the preserves of other parts of the Association in its endeavours to proselytise bear witness to both the zealous approach of committee members and to the impact which has been made.

Since it can no longer be taken for granted that the majority of librarians (even those in senior management positions) have more than a remote acquaintance with the details and problems of book construction – and this, more than anything else, differentiates the challenge facing the present Sub-committee from that faced by its predecessors – raising awareness amongst the professionals has had to take precedence over other activities. Such activity, however, could only be a first step in making friends and influencing people.

The change in the criteria for the award of prizes and medals clearly is one example of an instance where the Library Association has had a fairly direct impact on the activities of others. More indirect, but also effective, has been the pressure of various elements of the Association on publishers in other ways. The University, College and Research Section, in its regular meetings with the Publishers' Association has consistently pursued the question of acid-free paper. While it would be simple-minded to believe that this pursuit has been a primary contributor to publishers' changing attitudes, there can be no doubt, from the reaction of individual publishers present at such meetings, that, allied with similar pressures from other quarters, the discussions have had some impact.

The Library Association has also cooperated with the Publishers' Association and others in the production of a pamphlet by John Trevitt on acid-free paper,[22] while specific approaches to HMSO and local authorities have resulted in welcome alterations in recommended practices.

Training and education, as opposed to general awareness raising, have always been at the forefront of the Sub-committee's endeavours but it does take time to get specific programmes off the ground. Apart from a course on 'Conservation and the librarian' run successfully by Nicolas Barker in 1985, only in the last year or two has earlier planning borne fruit. With the assistance of sponsorship from Dunn & Wilson, the Continuing Education Department has run an annual travelling workshop for the past two years on preservation administration. Despite organisational difficulties on both occasions an analysis of the responses to the first workshop has been very encouraging. A more general conservation seminar was also scheduled for this year by the Continuing Education Department while Robin Price, another member of the Sub-committee, has agreed to direct a workshop on disaster planning in the autumn. The number of people reached by these initiatives is, of course, very much smaller than the number who might read a news item in the *Library Association record.* The strength of the educational effort, however, is that it has reached considerable numbers of people who might feel reluctant to expose their ignorance and limited level of involvement in gatherings designed for the experts.

In the long run the efforts of the Continuing Education Department can only be successful if they are complemented by the work of the library schools. I have already suggested that success here has not been total. Despite the best efforts of the Sub-committee it is clear that opposing pressures will ensure that many library schools continue to find it difficult to make room for conservation matters in their curricula. Even here, however, it would appear that the efforts of the Library Association have helped to assist those already predisposed in favour of preservation to incorporate elements of preservation teaching in their courses.

Future directions

I have suggested that, for the time being, the efforts of the Library Association, at least so far as its flag-ship, the Sub-committee on Preservation and Conservation is concerned, have ceased to make further progress. Providing that the Association treats the present hiatus merely as a time to gather breath no harm need ensue; but constant vigilance is necessary. In the past, a revival of interest every other decade may have been sufficient to keep the problems reasonably in the forefront of the professional conscience. For a time conservation and preservation were the flavour of the month and won a degree of attention and respect which enabled a small group of activists to make substantial progress in introducing acid-free paper and in recouping some of the ground lost in education terms. Fads and fashions change however, and it is possible to suspect that preservation has now had its turn in the professional limelight. In recent professional meetings, more immediate matters, such as performance indicators and plans for charging for services, have been demanding attention. It will be all too easy in the near future for preservation needs to sink out of sight.

If this danger is to be avoided the Association will need to take seriously the policy statement it agreed in 1987,[23] at the prompting of the Sub-committee, and to pursue those areas where continuing effort will be required because of the changing nature of the problems being faced. Concepts of bookbinding in the 1950s may no longer be relevant in a context of industrial techniques of the early 1990s. The Sub-committee has recognised this as a matter of concern and must pursue solutions with vigour.

Progress in coordination and cooperation are equally essential. The Association can play a major role here. Although it lacks powers of direction and resources to entice, its existence as an umbrella-type organisation for different specialisations and for all ranges of library types should give it a crucial part to play in promoting understanding, reducing conflicts and advancing practical achievement. How far this will be achieved depends as always upon individual effort within the corporate structure but it will also require both a breadth of vision and an attention to detail which are all too difficult to combine. The Library Association's support for the Newsplan project is a good example of successful cooperation. Blind adherence to the lauded but as yet unrealised advantages of Conspectus may be an equally good example of unprofitable cooperation.

The minutes of the Sub-committee reveal disappointingly numerous instances where ideas have been mooted only to fail for want of further action.

Some of these ideas have been overtaken by events; others may be beyond the scope of the Sub-committee or even the Library Association to pursue. The residue certainly could provide the Sub-committee with a sufficient field of endeavour for the next six years of its existence.

Notes

1. W A Munford *A history of the Library Association 1877–1977.* London: LA, 1976, p.80.
2. *Book construction.* London: LA, 1931.
3. E A Clough *Bookbinding for librarians.* London: Association of Assistant Librarians, 1957.
4. *The care of books and documents.* London: LA, 1972.
5. R Bowden *Sub-committee on Conservation.* Library Association papers: PDE.304, January 1981.
6. *Directory of British Associations 1967–68.* 2nd ed. Beckenham: CBD Research, 1967, p.149; *Directory of British Associations.* 8th ed. Beckenham: CBD Research, 1986, p.285.
7. I R M Mowat *A policy proposal for the conservation and control of bookstock in academic libraries.* In: *Journal of librarianship* 14, 1982, pp.266–278.
8. R Bowden *Sub-committee on Conservation.* Library Association papers: PDE.304, January 1981.
9. F W Ratcliffe and D Patterson, eds. *Preservation policies and conservation in British Libraries: report of the Cambridge University Library Conservation Project.* London: British Library, 1984.
10. Library Association, Professional Development and Education Committee, Sub-committee on Conservation *Minutes of the meeting on 18 March 1982.* Library Association papers: PDE.421, May 1982.
11. J Tomes *Scotland.* London: Benn, 1977, p.37.
12. Library Association, Library & Information Services Committee, Sub-committee on Conservation *Minutes of the meeting on 11 October 1983.* Library Association papers: LIBSC.113, November 1983, Minute 9.
13. Library Association, Library & Information Services Committe, Sub-committee on Preservation and Conservation *Minutes of the meeting on 23 March 1987.* Library Association papers: LIBSC.444, April 1987, Minute 12.
14. Library Association, Library & Information Services Committee, Sub-committee on Preservation and Conservation *Minutes of the meeting on 27 February 1986.* Library Association papers: LIBSC.329, April 1986, Minute 86/4.
15. Library Association, Library & Information Services Committee, Sub-committee on Preservation and Conservation *Minutes of the meeting on 23 March 1987* Library Association papers: LIBSC.444, April 1987, Minute 10.
16. J Trevitt *Why we should change to permanent paper.* In: *Library Association record* vol.86, 1984, p.469; D W G Clements *Preservation and library school education programmes.* In: *Library Association record* vol.88, 1986, pp.136–7; J Feather *Curriculum for the teaching of conservation.* In: *Library Association record* vol.88, 1986, pp.499–501.
17. *Education for conservation.* In: *Journal of librarianship,* 17, 1985, pp.73–105.
18. R E Palmer, ed. *Preserving the word: the Library Association Conference proceedings, Harrogate 1986.* London: LA, 1987.
19. J M Dureau and D W G Clements *Principles for the preservation and conservation of library materials.* The Hague: IFLA Section on Conservation, 1986.
20. National Preservation Office *Preservation: a survival kit.* London: British Library, 1986.
21. Library Association, Library & Information Services Committee, Sub-committee on Preservation and Conservation *Minutes of the meeting on 6 August 1987.* Library Association papers: SC.CONS.143, October 1987, Minutes 6.1, 6.3, 7.
22. J Trevitt *Permanent paper.* London: LA, PA, NPO, 1986.
23. Library Association *Preservation & conservation: policy statement.* London: LA, 1987.

Jean M Plaister

Library cooperation and interlending

The *Principles for the preservation and conservation of library material* published by IFLA in 1986[1] state that:

> The objectives of preservation policies in relation to library materials may be defined as:
>
> (a) to preserve the intellectual content of the information recorded by transfer to other media
> and/or
> (b) to preserve the original physical form of library and archive material in as intact and useable a form as possible.
>
> Not every library can, or will want to, preserve every item in its collection in its original form, and the establishing of policy priorities is a necessary prerequisite for any library undertaking such work.

I believe that the majority of librarians would subscribe to these principles. It is rather like the Frenchman who became a naturalised Englishman and when asked what this meant to him, replied that before, Waterloo was a defeat; now as an Englishman he was on the winning side!

I believe, however, to put it another way, that it is easy to fight for our principles but much more difficult to carry them out in our daily lives.

What, then, has library cooperation and inter-library lending to do with preservation? Is it not a contradiction in terms, highlighting the old dilemma between use and preservation? I would deny this, maintaining that library cooperation and interlending are closely involved with preservation. The purpose of my talk here today is to explain my reasons for this belief and to consider what is already being done and what could be done in the future to improve the situation.

I start from the premise that no library is self-sufficient in terms of the needs of its users. We all rely to a lesser or greater extent on inter-library lending and document supply, and here I would take these terms to be indistinguishable.

The source of the material required, and in most cases the form in which it is received, are immaterial to a reader. Although surveys show that most material obtained through inter-library loan is of fairly recent origin, long experience has shown me that it is virtually impossible to predict what material will be required. That is not to say, however, that we should not make greater efforts to estimate the extent of duplication required to meet present and future needs and to decide what material to preserve and which method to adopt.

We all rely on access to information on resources and the location of individual items. For interlending such information is vital. It ought to be possible to assume that a national library or a group of national libraries retain copies of their country's literary output. One copy, however, may well not be sufficient to meet the needs of users and few national libraries would claim to be all-embracing in their collections. The introduction of new technology into libraries and in particular the development of international standards and telecommunications which will enable system to talk to system (OSI – Open Systems Interconnection) will undoubtedly improve access to location information. Yet in another way, new technology has been the enemy rather than the friend of inter-library lending.

When I first became a librarian, in fact even when I began to work in the cooperation and interlending field, the choices were relatively simple. Library locations were recorded in manual union catalogues; in the UK these locations were entered in the Regional and/or National Central Library union catalogues. Material could either be lent through the interlending system or, if too frail or valuable, could be consulted in the host library. It was a relatively easy matter for libraries to produce an additional copy of a catalogue entry to send to the regional or national union catalogue.

In my early days at the Region, libraries would send us or bring in their catalogue cards to check if a potential withdrawal was the last copy within the Region; every effort was made to retain last copies either by the library itself or within the appropriate subject specialisation collection. Equally most libraries had a fairly clear policy of retention of older materials. It would be wrong of me of course, to suggest that this scheme was perfect – far from it. The maintenance of regional and national union catalogues absorbed an enormous amount of staff time, and success relied very much on conscientious librarians in participating libraries.

The development of shared cataloguing cooperatives in the nineteen sixties was an important advance. For as a by-product of their main activity, location lists and union catalogues could be produced for interlending and shared use of resources. BLCMP[2] for example sent and still sends LASER[3] a two-monthly magnetic tape of new titles added by LASER members for automatic addition to the LASER database which is now the union catalogue.

In recent years, suppliers have developed stand-alone systems. The records used within these local systems may not conform to MARC standards. Records are tailored to the needs of individual libraries, and provision of facilities in a local system for creating a union catalogue has not been seen as a high priority. OSI standards may provide for system to system access but unless this is backed up by a plan for cooperation in preservation future generations will not have access to resources.

In the good old days, possibly because less material was purchased, most libraries (and here I am particularly thinking about public libraries) had a fairly clear policy of retention of older materials. Experience has shown me that this is often no longer the case, and that many libraries have not come to terms with the complexity of the situation. New technology has not only revolutionised the recording of bibliographic records and locations but has radically expanded the type and form of materials in our libraries and the methods available for their preservation and duplication.

I want to spend a little time now speaking about NEWSPLAN[4] which is a very good example of the type of cooperation I am talking about. The aims and objectives of NEWSPLAN are to establish 'a programme maintained by the British Library and supported by other libraries for the preservation of UK local newspapers before 1985, with the British Library, local libraries, newspapers and other institutions working in cooperation to identify the problems and the priorities and to seek resources.'

The origin of the programme was a research proposal from the South Western Regional Library System in 1983 which was supported with a grant from the British Library Research and Development Department. It is hoped to extend the research to cover all the library Regions of the UK and the Republic of Ireland with similar projects to that undertaken in the South West. Already the North West, East Midlands, Northern, Yorkshire and Humberside regions have initiated NEWSPLAN projects, and the others apart from LASER and Scotland have a NEWSPLAN steering committee.

The research is funded jointly by the British Library and the Regions and aims to visit all collections in libraries, archives, newspaper offices and other bodies to assess the holdings and their state of physical preservation; to assess the volume and quality of microfilming done to date; to make recommendations for future microfilming programmes and to provide data from which these can be costed and planned; and to encourage the observation of good technical standards.

Newspapers are a vital source of local and social history, but since about 1860 newspapers have been printed on cheap wood-pulp based paper which is subject to deterioration. Some files have been lost completely and others are in very poor condition. Microfilm is the medium used to provide substitutes for the originals as it is the only proven technology yet available. From 1985 onwards the British Library is microfilming all newspapers which are not being microfilmed by other agencies, but Eve Johansson, Head, British Library Newspaper Library, estimates that to capture on microfilm all surviving newspaper files up to the year 1985 would require 350 camera years: that is, 35 specialist microfilm cameras fully occupied for 10 years. She believes that 'there is a need for a national structure and a national plan supported by the Regions, to encourage a continuing commitment to microfilming programmes and to monitor progress on the recommendations of the NEWSPLAN reports, and that the National Committee on Regional Library Cooperation is the most appropriate body to set this up.' I believe that there is every indication that this plan will be adopted. If this national plan is successful it would provide a precedent for similar programmes in other areas.

Some four or five years ago Maurice Line asked the Regions to look again at retention of last copies. Some Regions (eg LASER) still maintained partial if not comprehensive subject specialisation schemes, but gone were the days when staff were available to check last copies against the Regional union catalogue. The National Committee on Regional Library Cooperation referred Professor Line's suggestion to the Regions and the unanimous decision was that the proposals were unworkable.

Union catalogues were, however, being automated at the time, although online access was in its infancy, and this at least to me, provided hope for the future. Advances in technology during the past decade have revolutionised access to the database, and the regional union catalogue has taken advantage of these developments. The VISCOUNT service will have some 50 LASER members online by the end of the current financial year. In addition, the Regional Headquarters in the North West, South West and Scotland are online together with four or five test sites in each Region. It is early days, but online access could provide the basis for further 'last copy' research. The JANET network and the CURL initiative to produce a centralised index to holdings will provide a parallel development in the university and research library area.

It would be foolish to believe that these forms of 'preservation cooperation' will be easy. The adoption of OSI standards to allow computer to computer system communication will not be the answer to all our problems. Conformance testing to ensure that potential partners are interpreting these standards in the same way is essential. The National Library of Canada is carrying out conformance testing with selected libraries in Canada for the implementation of OSI ILL protocols, so there is hope.

The LISC (Library and Information Services Council) report *Future development of libraries 2. Working together within a national framework*[5] recommended centres of excellence and an 'access' strategy rather than 'collection' and the third report advocated the setting up of LIPs.[6] It is interesting to reflect however, that the recent Green Paper issued by the Office of Arts and Libraries on public library charges,[7] appears to threaten this 'access' strategy by suggesting that library authorities should charge one another for services including items lent on inter-library loan. There is also encouragement to impose economic charges on individual and corporate users. Although the consultative paper relates to public libraries, the implications could be far wider. As the Library Association says in its response to the consultative paper: 'It seems quite likely that an authority that decides not to charge will be reluctant to lend to one that does. Conversely, the financial burden on authorities which are net borrowers would be such as to challenge the voluntary nature of the proposals. The continued membership of non-public libraries of the interlending network, especially large academic libraries, which tend to be net lenders, also seems doubtful under the Green Paper's proposals. The result is likely to be a much less effective interlending system and reduced access to information and ideas.'[8]

I have ranged fairly widely over the field of library cooperation and interlending, but before I sum up I would like to deal briefly with nontraditional publishing. Here I am not just thinking about records, cassettes, videos and CD-ROMs, but electronic publishing and on-demand publishing.

These new developments are not just a problem to those involved in library cooperation and interlending of course, but they demonstrate the complexity of the situation which faces us all. The National Committee on Regional Library Cooperation has a Working Party on the Interlending of Non-Book Materials. This Working Party has produced a national 'non-book' interlending form and guidelines for the production of general subject directories. The work of creating union catalogues is hampered by lack of identifiable number (ie ISBN) or MARC type records.

Earlier in this paper, I spoke of the need not only to fight for our principles but to carry them out in our daily work. Our system of interlending and document supply is the envy of the world and we lead the way in preservation and conservation. In both these fields we also take a leading role in Europe. I believe it is important for us as librarians to persuade the government that cooperation in the shared use of resources through preservation and conservation is vital to a healthy library service. Then we must build on the NEWSPLAN concept in other areas and embrace the use of developing automation and telecommunications systems which can assist us in this work.

Preservation and conservation are inextricably linked with library cooperation and interlending.

Notes

1. J M Dureau and D W G Clements *Principles for the preservation and conservation of library materials.* The Hague: IFLA Section on Conservation, 1986.
2. BLCMP = Birmingham Libraries Cooperative Mechanisation Project.
3. LASER = London and South Eastern Library Region.
4. Rosemary Wells *NEWSPLAN: report of the pilot project in the South West.* London: British Library Research and Development Department (LIR 38), 1986.
5. Library and Information Services Council *The future development of libraries and information services 2. Working together within a national framework.* London: HMSO, 1982. (Library and Information Series No.12.)
6. Library and Information Services Council *The future development of libraries and information services: progress through planning and partnership.* London: HMSO, 1986. (Library and Information Series No.14.)
7. *Financing our public library service: four subjects for debate: a consultation paper.* London: HMSO, 1988, Cmnd 324.
8. The Library Association *Response to 'Financing our public library service: four subjects for debate' Cmnd 324.* London: Library Association, 1988.

Terry Cannon

A review of the new technologies

I should like to talk about two main effects of technology on libraries and preservation:

(1) how it could affect coverage and acquisition policies;

(2) how it could provide possible solutions to preservation problems.

I have used conditional phraseology because the situation at present is very unpredictable and likely to remain so for the forseeable future; many of the technologies, and their ultimate place in the scheme of things are as yet neither proven technically nor accepted in the market place.

Technology and the production of materials

Since the invention of printing from moveable type by Gutenberg in the fifteenth century, paper has proliferated; and print on paper is still the favoured means of dissemination of well over 90 per cent of information. For most publishers, 'electronic publication' means the electronic means to handle and speed the process of producing a printed book. It has already made possible great increases in efficiency and output, and will lead to parallel and quite new publications in other forms, of which more later, but these are still in their infancy. (Similarly, automation of offices appears to have led to far more printed products rather than less.)

Desk Top Publishing (DTP) has rapidly acquired a popularity which will alarm or excite the more assiduous collectors of printed material. The availability of cheap scanners, microcomputers, software intermediate between word-processing and photocomposing software and high quality laser printers lures many would-be authors, and small organisations, into 'being their own publisher'. The problems for libraries of identifying, selecting, acquiring, controlling and preserving such output will be considerable. Not all of it is of high quality – the discipline and design and composition skills required were not appreciated by many users driven on by the producers' enticing advertisements – and much is ephemeral, yet a great deal will still need to be collected and retained in major libraries, especially as experience increases and micro systems become more powerful and sophisticated. The British Library is at this moment putting out a contract to investigate the likely impact of DTP trends on its collection policies, as an adjunct to Dr Enright's study of collection and retention policies.

It is possible, however, that in the longer term, print-on-paper will decrease in absolute as well as in relative terms. True electronic publishing implies electronic input, handling and output – the whole publication chain as discussed in Priscilla Oakeshott's BNBRF report *From author to reader.*[1] Are libraries equipped to acquire and preserve the non-print products of electronic publishing? Some of the issues are raised in a perceptive article by Paul Sturges[2] and earlier discussions on the subject are covered comprehensively in a BNBRF report by Susan Hills.[3] To acquire only the paper versions of a publication may have been a viable policy in the past. It will become a restrictive and ultimately self-defeating one as more and more information is available only in electronic database form. This has been happening for a long time with abstracting and indexing services, whose parallel printed publications often contain less data, and is increasingly the case with reference works such as directories and encyclopedias. How much longer, for example, will printed rail timetables and telephone directories be available?

Another source of material that may, or may not, find its way into libraries stems from the increasing use of electronic networks for academic communications and the formation of 'invisible colleges'. JANET, for example, supports electronic mail, conference systems and bulletin boards, such as HUMBUL. Much of the information exchanged is in very small units and at a low level, though some may find its way into published articles and books eventually. The BLEND project[4] showed that such systems were well suited to short communications but that for a full electronic journal, substantial contributions required considerable effort. Higher capacity transmission lines and greater facilities for handling text and graphics will encourage a trend to exchange more substantial data.

Nevertheless, there is already in certain disciplines an unquantified amount of material of primary importance, which is only held electronically and only accessible to those in the know. When articles are printed out, it is often difficult to know if they are the definitive version, and how they should be handled bibliographically. The bypassing of any formal publishing and archiving process *could* mean that the information age will leave very little trace of itself for posterity. The advantage of formal publication lies in providing both a check on quality and a channel to libraries and the wider market.

But this possible loss of information is probably the reverse of the nightmare experienced by many managers of collections, and that is the need to handle the many and varied artifacts of electronic dissemination:

– magnetic tapes and discs in a bewildering variety of formats and standards, requiring many machines and programs to manifest their content

– audio material
The National Sound Archive collections include everything from wax cylinders (and their players) to compact digital disc and digital audio tape

– visual and audio-visual material
photographs, film, videotape, videodisc CD-Video and CD-I

– mixed media material
such as text books with computer software or cassettes

– computer based instruction with associated printed material, manuals, illustrations etc.

One development that has long been anticipated is the appearance of the electronic book: portable, machine readable, as easy to use as a book and in as many places. In Australia, the 'Smartbook' is being developed, and consists of a 9 × 6 × 1¼ inch reader with LCD screen and six control buttons, taking a 1 Mb credit card size book on ROM. About 4–5 Mb can actually be encoded by compression techniques, including text, index and search functions. The initial market is for professional reference works but as technology gets cheaper and sales increase, the consumer market will be attacked.

Perhaps only a few libraries or archives need to conserve the whole range of media, and, perhaps, become museums of the technology. Yet comprehensive subject content and coverage can often only be achieved by including such items and publication of serious works increasingly becomes a mixed media affair. If we are lucky, technology will itself come to the rescue, and with improved standards and automated conversion will permit retention in only a few of the many possible media.

As an example, the ESRC Data Archive has probably the most highly developed expertise in handling machine-readable records. Since 1967, it has collected over 2,500 files on social and economic matters, mainly government, academic and commercial surveys. These files are accessible via JANET on line. In soliciting data, it sets technical conditions and insists on full documentation, to ensure that the data can be fully used. Much data was repackaged into the Domesday disc. The Archive relies on the 'Shell' concept, with data converted to an in-house format. This is costly, but if there is any change of computer technology, a single overall conversion can be made; this has successfully been achieved over three generations of computer hardware. The Archive's success lies in being pro-active: in telling depositors what is wanted, putting effort into maximising usefulness, and specialising in one type of data. The meassage is: be selective.

Technology as an aid to preservation

Since the advent of microfilm, technology has offered the possibility of both reducing the volume and also preserving the information content of archived materials in a simple process. To summarise Tony Hendley's 1982 report,[5] most of which still obtains:

paper, if of good quality and acid-free is still the safest bet, while newer technologies have still to prove themselves.

microfilm of archive quality has a guaranteed life of 50 years and is compact, but difficult for retrieval and unpopular with users.

magnetic media are unstable, require frequent refreshment and are prone to damage through the read-write mechanisms. Although compact and fast of access, they are hardware and software dependent and become obsolete.

optical media may well be the answer, and are being actively and extensively investigated.

It seems appropriate here to discuss optical media in more detail. They all rely on laser technology for recording and reading, offer very high storage capacity, employ no mechanical contact and provide good, fast retrieval and apparent durability. Inevitably, a variety of forms, formats, physical media, software and players have been produced and experimented with, and it is an advantage to wait a little, while market forces sort out the rival systems and industry gets its act together. Trends are emerging, and while libraries may not have the influence to dictate final outcomes, they are not without some power. Certainly, production of the British Library's first CD-ROM[6] met with willing cooperation from Philips, enabling it to be ready in a mere six weeks in time for the 1985 Frankfurt Book Fair. Inclusion of *British books in print* led to subsequent agreement between Whitakers and Philips to produce *Bookbank,* with a monthly update cycle.

CD-ROM does seem to be establishing a foothold in our area, undoubtedly carried on the back of the success of audio compact disc. The adoption of the 'High Sierra' standard means that most discs will now play on most players and the 'read only' aspect protects publishers from illegal copying. CD-ROM is ideal for medium-size data bases (eg *Eighteenth century short title catalogue* and *British books in print*); reference works (eg Grolier *Encyclopedia, Oxford English dictionary*); maps (eg *Supermap,* Australian census data) and text and pictures (eg ADONIS, medical records[7]). It is being used most effectively with custom-built search software and appropriately structured contents. Several hundred products are now available, mostly in the United States. The interest in and use of CD-ROM in Italy, with its well-known telecommunications problems, suggests applications in third world countries. No doubt CD-ROM will be superseded, but it should enjoy several years' pre-eminence.

CD-I, which allows combinations of data, sound and graphics, and DVI, using advanced compression techniques to record up to an hour of full motion video on compact disc, are really a subset of CD-ROM technology and aimed mainly at the entertainment market. Although long-heralded, they have been slow to emerge, and manufacturers are clearly having technical problems in meeting the specification. Recently, the production of CD-I has been put back to next year.[8]

CD-ROM can only be mastered and manufactured in a small number of places, although capacity for stamping copies is now well able to cope with demand. WORM (write once, read many) systems allow customers to write their own data and build up archives on a disc, offering better long-term prospects. WORM is available in 5¼-inch, 12-inch and 14-inch format (DIP systems), the latter particularly aimed at the office market and large organisations, but libraries may benefit from falling prices as office automation systems proliferate (*eg* Filenet, Megadoc).

There are many areas of the British Library collection that could, over the next ten years, require digitised image storage, including maps, the oriental collections, manuscripts and the Title Room. Hugh Wilman is to investigate and report on the various optical disc systems that are available for archival purposes. Pilot projects will be devised with a view to implementing live systems in St Pancras.

Laser disc systems have probably been around longest but made little impact on the consumer market; exploiting their large capacity (56,000 pictures) and high quality has been an expensive pioneering effort. Nevertheless there have been many applications in educational areas exploiting their interactive possibilities and also in photographic archives.

The Domesday project is an imaginative and interesting application showing the versatility and range of material they can hold and offering some interesting search analysis and mapping techniques, but it shows there is much work still to be done. A major problem is the need for research on information retrieval from large image banks (*eg* graphical search keys, coding by various facets etc). The various sizes in which laser discs come (12 cm, 5¼-inch, 12-inch, 14-inch), even if dictated by applications, do illustrate at a simple level, the standards problem. At the individual book-size level, the Laser-card (*eg* Drexler) could become popular, holding one Mb of information and up to ten with compression, since all seem to conform to credit card size. However, libraries will have security problems if they stock such items and may need to install vending machines.

Erasable optical discs have been announced and shown by Thompson Grand Public.[9] Various coatings, dyes, phase change or magneto-optic effects and substrates are the subject of experiments, mainly in Japan (*eg* Fujitsu). These are probably more suitable and useful for computer storage than for archives, but applications may suggest themselves.

Optical tape allows data to be recorded using optical techniques. One version is being marketed by ICI under the confusing name 'digital paper'. For retrieval it suffers from the disadvantage common to all tape systems of serial search/long search times, although it can hold a colossal amount of data in very compact form, making it a useful back-up system. Creo Electronics tape drive can hold 2,400 feet of ½-inch opt tape (1 Tera byte = 10^{12} bytes); access in approximately 30 seconds is claimed.[10]

DAT has similar capacity (about one Gb) but its main threat to CD is consumer preference: because it is recordable, collapse of the CD market could follow.

Although optical discs have been heralded as the archival medium of the future, Hendley[5] pointed out as long ago as 1982 that their longevity is unproven. Manufacturers have claimed minimum lifetimes ranging from ten to a hundred years, but Barry Fox, writing in the *New scientist*[11] has discovered flaws in the manufacture of CDs which cast considerable doubt. The principal problem seems to be that the ink used on the labels etches through the lacquer, allowing air in to oxidise the aluminium layer on which the digital information is recorded, which then becomes non-reflecting. Very small imperfections can be overcome by the error-correcting software, but beyond a certain threshold the whole disc becomes unreadable. Philips and Nimbus have issued statements denying the use of the offending ink on their discs, and blaming poor quality discs produced by cost-cutting competitors. Another problem could be caused by molecular creep (migration of atoms of metal across the surface into and out of, and ultimately smoothing out, the tiny pits recording the information). Silver, gold and even platinum are being tried to give a harder, less corrodible reflecting layer, but such discs will be much more expensive. Because compact discs have only been in existence for a few years, nobody really knows their true lifetime. Tests conducted so far are of 'accelerated ageing', subjecting discs to a regime of extremes of heat, humidity and mechanical fatigue. The British Library is setting up tests at the National Sound Archive on WORM discs and CD-ROM using a number of different makes of disc and disc drive. Results will be available in about one year's time.

Although the message of the foregoing could be summarised as 'caveat emptor', I would not like to close on too gloomy a note. While technology has undoubtedly increased the volume and range of materials to be archived and preserved, it will also offer compact, retrievable means of storage. The library and archive world needs to concern itself with standards of manufacture and production to ensure that its more rigorous specifications are met.

Notes

For all aspects of disc technology and its applications, CIMTECH at Hatfield Polytechnic is a most useful source of information.

1. P Oakeshott *The impact of new technology on the publication chain.* BNBRF Report 11. London: British Library, 1983. ISBN 0 7123 3007 0.
2. P Sturges *Policies and criteria for the archiving of electronic publishing.* In: *Journal of librarianship* vol.19, no.3 July 1987.
3. S Hills *Archival aspects of electronic publications and their availability.* BNBRF Report. London: British Library, 1983.
4. B Shackel and D Pullinger *BLEND-1: background and developments.* LIR Report 29. London: British Library, 1984. ISBN 0 7123 3042 9.
5. A Hendley *The archival potential of microfilm, magnetic media and optical discs.* BNBRF Report 10. CIMTECH: Hatfield Polytechnic, 1982.
6. A Clarke *The British Library's compact disc experiment.* London: British Library 1986. ISBN 0 7123 3086 0.
7. *Medical information system on WORM disc from 3M.* In: *Optical data systems* vol.3, no.5, p.6 May 1988.
8. *CD is not all fun and games* In: *The Times* 28 June 1988.
9. *Optical disk materials.* In: *Reprographic technologies bulletin* issue 1 February 1988 and *Erasable optical disc player, ibid* issue 4 May 1988.
10. Report on AIIM 77 Exhibition. In: *Optical data systems* vol.3, no.5, p.4 May 1988.
11. B Fox *Tests prove CDs can self destruct* In: *New scientist* 7 July 1988.

Mary Wilkinson

Optical disks at the Public Record Office: a summary

This paper will discuss the circumstances that led to the Public Record Office, a very small department in government terms, becoming involved in 'leading edge technology' for the first time in its history.

I should first explain a little about the function of the Public Record Office, or PRO. The PRO is the national archive for the records of the United Kingdom government and Courts of Law. All records created in government which are considered to be of historical value are selected for permanent preservation and transferred to the PRO where they are made available to the public when they become 'open' after thirty years, or later depending upon their content and sensitivity. Some examples of the types of record held are: Domesday Book, the most famous record, Magna Carta, and more recently Cabinet Office minutes, War Office records, the Census etc. In total, the PRO holds more than 86 miles of records in its offices at Kew and Chancery Lane in London.

Up till now all these records have been on paper, parchment or microfilm, with a small number of sound and film recordings. However, we had been aware for a number of years that this situation was changing rapidly and that records in machine readable form had been selected for preservation at the PRO. At the moment the records in question are digitally encoded and held on magnetic tape; they tend to contain survey and statistical data. In the longer term it is possible that most records will be transferred in some sort of machine readable form, *eg* text and image. Examples of the types of files that could eventually be held are the Department of Health and Social Security file of the insured population, computerised versions of the Census etc.

As I mentioned, this situation has not come upon us as a complete surprise: we have been attempting to find a solution to the new problems created by transfer of such data for some time. The drawbacks to accepting magnetic tape into an archive, as we saw it, were:

1. the accommodation cost of storing an ever-increasing number of reels of tape

2. the staff cost of maintaining tapes according to the government code of practice

3. the cost of environmental controls

4. the risk of amendment or deletion of data

Nevertheless we had to seek a solution, as it was becoming increasingly difficult to persuade creating departments to continue to bear the cost of maintaining the tapes that had been selected for permanent preservation. We therefore drew up plans to establish a data archive based on magnetic tape and these plans were discussed both with CCTA (Central Computer and Telecommunications Agency) and HM Treasury, who turned them down mainly on the grounds of cost. HM Treasury found the idea of funding the maintainance of an ever increasing tape library quite unacceptable.

We had during this time continued to liaise with CCTA in finding alternative technical solutions and in 1980 we became aware of optical disk technology which we believed looked promising for the future. Development took rather longer than anticipated but eventually in 1985 advice from CCTA was that the product was now sufficiently established to merit pilot testing. CCTA had already done some early work using optical disk which looked encouraging and which promised substantial savings for data storage compared with magnetic tape. In an experiment carried out in conjunction with the Property Services Agency, CCTA reported that they copied 62 files from the tape library to one side of an optical disk: the implications even for cutting accommodation costs therefore looked encouraging[1] CCTA then formed an Optical Disk Working Group made up of representatives of government departments with an interest in archival storage and it was agreed that government must acquire demonstrator systems in order fully to evaluate the technology. The PRO decided to approach HM Treasury to fund such a project and HM Treasury agreed that the product justified evaluation in view of the potential savings to the whole of government if it proved suitable.

In March 1986 the PRO issued an operational requirement to a number of suppliers for the supply of hardware and software to run an Optical Disk Pilot Project. The procurement followed normal government guidelines and a contract was awarded to Data General Ltd in September 1986 for supply of the total system. This system was installed in the PRO at Kew in March 1987 and comprised:

Hardware: A Data General MV4DC mini computer with 2Mb memory, 120Mb magnetic disk, 1 Cipher 2Gb optical disk drive, 2 consoles and a printer. Media was supplied by 3M.

Software: The software was specially written for the PRO by Data General and is best illustrated by showing the top level system menu, as follows:

PRO Optical Disk System
Main Menu

1. File Analysis	(Display and print blocks from a file)
2. File Transfer	(Transfer a file from one medium to another)
3. Compare Files	(Compare files on different media)
4. Maintain Index	(Maintain, Enquire, Print cumulative index)
5. Maintain File Layouts	(Maintain, Print file layout descriptions)
6. Optical Disk	(Optical Disk utilities)

Enter choice: ____

To exit, press the CANCEL/EXIT key – for more information press HELP key.

Training of two staff in system operation then followed. Owing to a shortage of staff with IT skills these staff came to the project from non-technical backgrounds. It was therefore a major requirement that the system could be used by such staff. It has proved to be a successful solution: we have staff running the project who are already highly knowledgeable about PRO records and procedures, and who are now learning how to cope with the problems presented by a new type of record.

Live running of the system will continue till the end of 1988, when we will evaluate its performance. So far nothing has happened to dampen our enthusiasm for optical disk technology, and the results look encouraging. Having established that the technology does enable us to store and retrieve data successfully, our main purpose now is to attempt to establish confidence in the media itself. We therefore already carry out regular integrity checking and comparisons, but are now about to go one stage further.

In conjunction with Data General, Cipher, CCTA and NPL we have established a Media Integrity Working Group whose aim has been to identify problems that could occur with the media and then to initiate a programme of monitoring to detect any such problems at the earliest possible opportunity. This programme will include such checks as physical measurement of disks, inspection of plastic surfaces, electromicroscopic scanning and read verification.

We now regard this as the most important aspect of the project. It is premature to say that the pilot project is a success but I believe we will establish a data archive using optical disk if only because it is the most suitable medium around at the present time.

To summarise, we believe the benefits are:

1. non-erasable media, which is ideal for archival purposes

2. improved life cycle for data, even if not permanent

3. cost savings over magnetic storage

Note

1. HM Treasury *Information technology in the civil service: data storage on optical disk – an experiment.* IT Series No.13.

Cliff McKnight

Electronic document delivery

Abstract

This paper describes the ADONIS document delivery system in relation both to its intended purpose and to its possible usage. The potential of such systems is then discussed in relation to the 'scholarly communication' framework of Project Quartet.

Introduction

The term Electronic Document Delivery (EDD), like the term Electronic Publishing (EP), tends to have two distinct meanings: one the use of electronic technology to support the delivery of a paper-based product; the other the delivery and use of a document in purely electronic form. In this sense, electronic document delivery is as much about reading from screens as it is about facsimile transmission.

In this paper I will use both meanings of EDD since both are important in the modern world. Although there is increasing use of technology to support (or, some would say, fuel) the information revolution, it is clear that paper-based documents will be used for some considerable time to come. As a psychologist, I am interested in how people make use of technology and how the technology might be made more usable. For the most part, people use electronic document technology to perform some task which was previously performed using paper-based media. Hence, rather than see the two uses of the term EDD as separate, I am interested in exploring the relationship between them.

In order to provide a focus for the paper, I will concentrate on the ADONIS document delivery system since it embodies many of the features which would seem to be required of an EDD system. However, I will also speculate on how such a system could be extended to support a wider range of user tasks, using the 'scholarly communication' framework of Project Quartet.

The ADONIS system

The idea behind the ADONIS project was that if information technology could be used to fulfil document requests at a lower cost than current photocopier-based methods, the savings could be used to increase the copyright holder's revenue without affecting the cost of the document to the supply centre or the end user. Hence, not unnaturally for a project funded by a consortium of publishers, the motivation behind ADONIS was financial rather than what might be termed research-orientated'.

The workstation finally assembled is built around an IBM PC/AT or compatible machine. To this reasonably powerful desktop microcomputer is added a CD-ROM drive, a high resolution A4 screen and a laser printer.

A total of 219 biomedical journals are digitally scanned, the number of articles being sufficient to merit the production of one CD-ROM per week. The articles are held in bit image format on the CD-ROM and can be viewed on the screen or, more normally, simply sent to the laser printer to produce a good-quality copy.

The software provided with the workstation allows an operator to enter a number of document requests and then automatically groups the requests to form a print queue according to the contents of the individual CD-ROMs. This is intended to minimise the need to keep changing the CD-ROM since the drive can only hold one at a time. The prospect of switching between 100 CD-ROMs might seem a little daunting, but 'juke-boxes' capable of holding many CD-ROMs are being investigated. Also, it is worth remembering the current method – walking through many yards of shelving!

In this respect, then, the ADONIS system offers the potential for efficient large-scale storage and rapid retrieval of journal articles. Furthermore, the quality of the output from the laser printer compares reasonably favourably with a photocopy of the article.

ADONIS: other possible uses

Although designed specifically for use in document supply centres, with the printed article being posted to the requester, other uses could be made of the ADONIS system. It is such uses that I will consider in this section.

For example, the articles are stored on the CD-ROM in a bit-mapped facsimile format. Hence, rather than being printed on a printer next to the microcomputer, the article could be transmitted to a remote facsimile machine for printing. In this way information technology could be used to replace the paper-based postal system. Indeed, experiments based on such an idea have been conducted in collaboration with the British Library Document Supply Centre by Dr Bill Tuck with some success.

Additionally, communications technology might allow the sending of document requests electronically, even over the relatively slow Joint Academic Network (JANET). It is only when an entire article is to be transmitted that high-speed lines become a necessity. However, it is not difficult to imagine a 'mixed speed' system whereby a researcher sends an electronic request to a supply centre using JANET and the article is transmitted to a facsimile machine in the researcher's campus library.

Rather than restrict use of the system to document supply centres, the workstation could be made available directly to end users. The resolution of the screen and the scanned image are sufficient to allow reading and browsing of the article, with printing of the entire article still possible if necessary. In this way, users could have direct rapid access to a large database of articles.

In order to determine whether end users could make effective use of the ADONIS system, we have been conducting trials with a major London medical library. Here, the service has been advertised to a large group of potential users who have been able to use the system at any time during normal office hours, with the added bonus that no charge has been made for the printing of articles during the trial period. We are not yet able to give the outcome of the trials, but they are due to end in a month's time and results will be published by early next year.

Future systems: the Project Quartet perspective

The ADONIS system was designed for a particular use and any evaluation of it must be primarily in relation to its suitability for that use. In Project Quartet we have an interest in document delivery but from the wider perspective of 'scholarly communication'. It is interesting, therefore, to consider ADONIS-like systems in relation to this wider perspective, to investigate their potential uses as we are doing in the medical library, and so forth. With this in mind, what follows should not be seen as implied criticism of the ADONIS system.

If we consider how the present-day scholar communicates, such methods as journal articles, books, conference papers and seminars spring to mind. Within Project Quartet we have been interested in the impact of information technology on this communication process, assuming that increasing use will be made of such technology. We have been concerned to investigate the extent to which the technology supports current activities as well as opening up new avenues of communication.

To guide our thinking, we can envisage a 'scholar's workstation' which would look superficially similar to the ADONIS workstation. For example, such a system could sensibly be based on a powerful desk-top microcomputer like the IBM PC/AT or the Apple Macintosh II; it would have a large-volume local storage device such as a CD-ROM drive; and it would have a large, high-resolution screen. How, then, might we change the ADONIS system into a Quartet system?

CD-ROM related changes

As was stated earlier, the journal articles are stored on the CD-ROM in the form of bit-mapped images. In crude terms, this means that for each pixel of the screen, a note is made of whether it should be 'on' or 'off'. Hence, although a human might recognise the pattern of dots as forming letters and words, to the computer they are simple on-off decisions. This means that the text of an article cannot be searched – it can only be displayed a page at a time. Where the primary intention is to print the entire article, the decision to hold the images as bit-maps is entirely reasonable. However, if the reader wants to search for a particular term or extract selected passages it is necessary to hold the text in a different format – usually in what is known as ASCII (American Standard Code for Information Interchange) format. Unfortunately, while ASCII format is designed for alphanumeric characters, it cannot represent graphics without resorting to fairly complicated coding techniques. Hence, if the scholar is to have searchable text and graphics, the documents need to be stored on the CD-ROM in some mixed format, possibly a mixture of ASCII and bit-maps or possibly using a page description language such as PostScript.

The CD-ROMs produced for ADONIS hold the contents of some 219 journals in the biomedical field. While this number is only a subset of the journals held by a medical library, it represents far more than the average scholar would access on a regular basis. Since we envisage the scholar's workstation to be used by an individual, it would be more sensible for the CD-ROMs to contain only those journals of direct relevance to the individual. Hence, a scholar would have a personal library of CD-ROMs containing only those books and journals of particular interest. Although current production costs do not allow it, we can envisage a 'subscription agency' producing individually tailored CD-ROMs on a regular basis.

Screen changes

If we look at the average scholar's desk, it seldom contains a single document. Even if the scholar is reading a document, the chances are that other documents will be open simultaneously, a notepad might be close at hand, and the telephone can ring at any time. Hence, if the scholar's workstation is to support at least current patterns of activity, it must be capable of displaying more than one document or task at a time. In terms of the display device required, then, it would seem that an A3 screen is preferable.

Connectivity changes

One of the most important features of the scholar's workstation is its connection to the 'outside world'. Rather than simply communicating with a printer, the scholar needs to communicate with colleagues and peers. Increasing use is being made of electronic mail, but Project Quartet has also been interested in the possible uses of computer-based conferencing systems. It is clear that such systems cannot provide all the same functions which present-day conferences provide – a brief poll of why scholars go to conferences produces a variety of responses like 'I like to travel' and 'All the real work is done in the bar in the evening'. However, in terms of information sharing, computer-based conferences have the specific advantage that participants do not need to be in the same place at the same time.

It is also interesting to speculate how the electronic scholar of the future will be connected to other information resources. The present structure (see

Figure 1) consists of the scholar having a personal store of information and, along with other scholars, making use of a local store (*eg,* campus library). Information not available here can be requested from a national library. Scholars can also request information directly from colleagues, and can use mail facilities to send information to colleagues and the library, but extensive discussion usually requires physical movement.

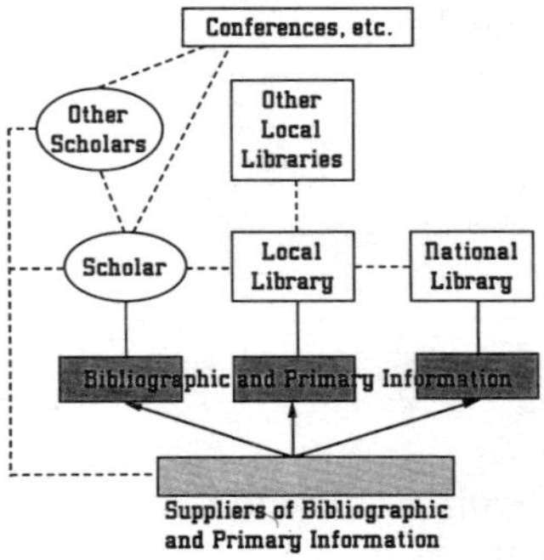

Figure 1: The current situation

By way of contrast, suppose we reduce the system to its essentials and consider a 'network of scholars' (see Figure 2). In this scenario, anyone who does not make a direct contribution to the end use of the information is removed – a return to the renaissance situation where each scholar had a personal library containing all known knowledge. Such a system would have the advantage of a high access 'bandwidth' – a lot of information can be transmitted from storage mechanism to user in a short space of time – but would create much duplication and be weak in terms of group communication.

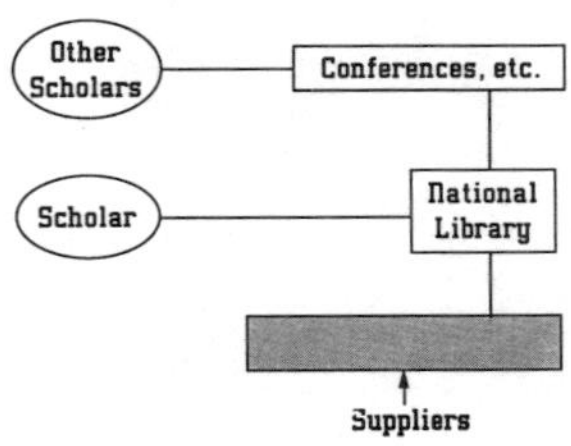

Figure 2: A network of scholars

As an alternative, consider a centralised system (see Figure 3). Here, all the information would be stored in one national archive which also provided mail and conferencing facilities. This would have the advantage of no duplication (other than for security backup purposes) and information would only be delivered when required. After all, the average number of readers per journal article is known to be small. However, access to such a system is likely to be a problem. It would require a very large number of high bandwidth lines or be non-interactive. It would also be very inefficient if a group of scholars in the same location (*eg,* a class of students) were accessing the same information at approximately the same time.

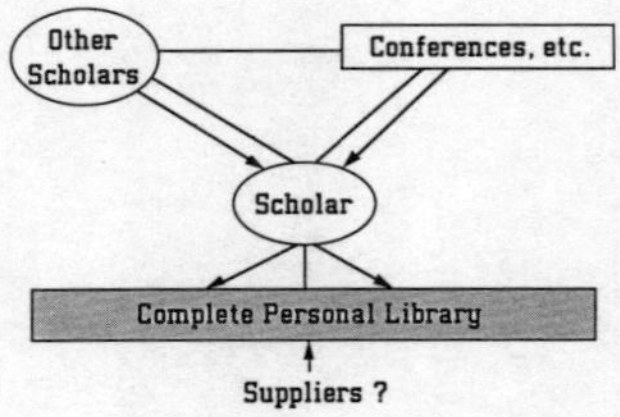

Figure 3: A centralised network

If we remove the national archive and distribute the primary and bibliographic material to local area networks (LANs), the system might look like that shown in Figure 4. Obviously, each LAN would not contain all the stored documents since this would approximate to a large number of centralised systems. However, it would allow particular LANs to specialise in material relevant to local needs. Obviously, though, the system would also need to support inter-LAN transfer, although this might be infrequent, low bandwidth transfers.

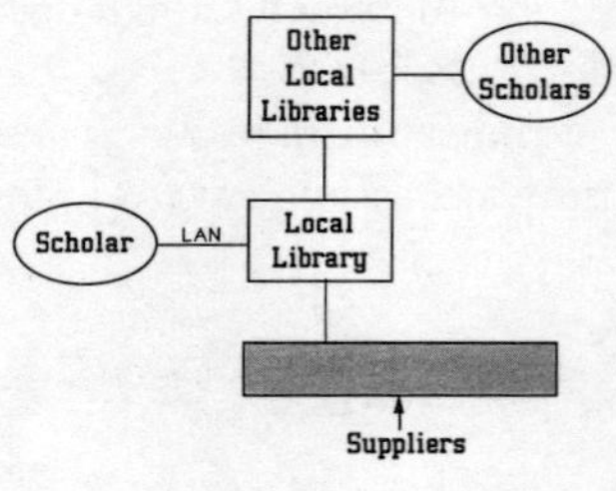

Figure 4: A distributed network

The three speculative scenarios represent 'extreme' cases which we can see as defining the limits of the possible systems. It is quite likely that in real life a hybrid system will develop which incorporates various pragmatic considerations. However, all three have implications not only for the way in which a scholar might work but also for the storage and transmission of information.

Conclusions

A project like ADONIS is interesting because it demonstrates ways in which information technology can be used to store and retrieve information. As such, it provides partial answers to some of the wider questions posed by Project Quartet. Electronic document delivery is clearly possible in a variety of ways. However, some thought must be given not only to the storage mechanisms like CD-ROMs but also the routes over which it is feasible or desirable to deliver the documents, since the routes chosen may have implications for the long-term archiving of information.

Acknowledgement
This work was carried out as part of Project Quartet, funded by the British Library Research and Development Department.

C E Butler, D W G Clements and C A Millington

Paper strengthening at the British Library: recent developments in the graft copolymerisation technique

Introduction

The importance of maintaining a programme for the conservation of library material is reflected in the estimated value of the library's collections. The British Library's central book collections are estimated to be worth in the order of £1,000 million; this is apart from the large and valuable collections of manuscripts. These are conservatively estimated to be worth a further £10,000 million.

To date there is a preservation backlog of some two million items, which would require conservation work costing £150 million. This figure increases by some £3 million every year as more books fall into the conservation category.

It has been generally accepted that the main cause of the deterioration of paper is the acid-catalysed hydrolysis of the cellulose. This reaction reduces the fibre length and hence the paper's strength and flexibility. Alum rosin sizing, atmospheric pollution and the use of poorly purified wood pulp have proved to be the main sources of acids. Other degradation processes such as oxidation (the by-products of oxidation can produce coloured products), occur simultaneously with acid degradation. The approach by conservators to this problem has been to neutralise the acid and leave a buffer against further acid attack. Unfortunately the methods used are labour intensive and expensive.

Therefore the need for low-priced bulk treatment processes has been realised by many countries. Deacidification by chemical means has been one of the options considered, and both the Public Archives of Canada and the Library of Congress have gone a long way to achieving this goal. The method based on the Wei T'o[1] process is the only one in commercial operation at present, although the French are also bringing a similar process into service in the near future. The Library of Congress has recently had a feasibility study done on the diethyl zinc method[2] and is now proceeding with further pilot plant studies. A recent review on the various deacidification options is presented in a report by George Cunha.[1]

Although the above processes are effective at neutralising the acid present and buffering against further acid attack, they do not specifically strengthen weakened paper fibres. Figures suggest that in some American collections up to 25 per cent of the book stock has fold values of one or less; while in the British Library only 7–9 per cent of the books fall into this fold category. These figures represent a large proportion of books which require immediate treatment and are particularly suitable for strengthening processes if they are to remain usable. An ideal conservation treatment would both stop acid attack and strengthen the weakened paper fibres. One approach to this problem has been developed for the British Library by the Industrial Chemistry Group, at the University of Surrey.

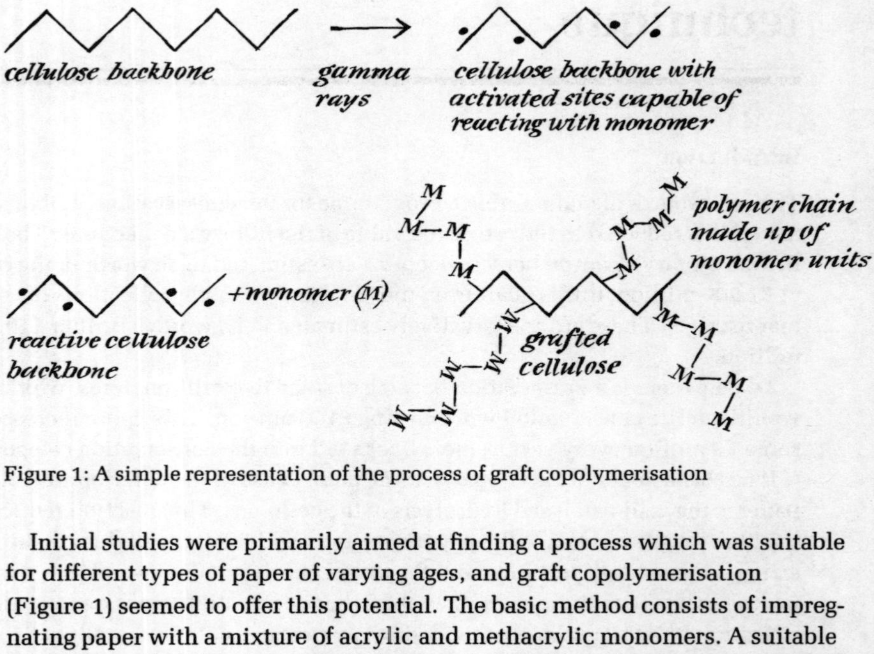

Figure 1: A simple representation of the process of graft copolymerisation

Initial studies were primarily aimed at finding a process which was suitable for different types of paper of varying ages, and graft copolymerisation (Figure 1) seemed to offer this potential. The basic method consists of impregnating paper with a mixture of acrylic and methacrylic monomers. A suitable mixture was found to be ethyl acrylate:methyl methacrylate in a 5:1 ratio. Other monomer components can be added to this basic mixture to impart specific end properties to the polymer/paper composite *eg* a basic monomer which effectively deacidifies prior to being polymerised. The samples are left to equilibrate to ensure an even distribution of monomer through the page and the book. Polymerisation is initiated by the use of low intensity gamma rays, which are particularly suitable for penetrating whole volumes. The end result is a paper/polymer composite in which some of the polymer is chemically attached to the cellulose – the major component of paper. Early work gave encouraging results with a variety of paper types, with strength increases of 5–10 times for papers containing 15–20 per cent by weight of polymer deposited in them

(Table 1), and resistance to acid attack was observed. Several patents on this work have now been granted.[3,4]

Table 1
Weight increases and fold endurance values for a variety of different substrates

Substrate	*Date*	*% Weight increase*	*Fold Endurance*	
			Control	*Treated*
Book K (Rag)	1839	24.4	13	119
Book I (Rag)	1838	19.4	80	1631
Book E (Esparto Mixture)	1874	24.7	8	48
Book F (Esparto Mixture)	1889	16.1	14	227
Book L (Esparto Mixture)	1903	23.1	9	328
Book DD (Mechanical)	1965	20.6	62	103
Chemical (no lignin)	1982/ 1983	24.6	175	3158
Chemimechanical (lignin present)	1982/ 1983	22.9	295	774

35% by weight monomer addition
Ethyl acrylate: methyl methacrylate 5:1
Total irradiation dose = 0.4 Mrad at a dose rate of 0.03 Mrad/h.

The next stage was to test whole volumes for suitability. This work also gave promising results and led to pilot plant studies. These are designed to give data which will enable a complete brief for commercial operation to be written.

Pilot plant studies

The first stage of this work consisted of designing a treatment container which could take five or more books in any of the desired orientations (Figure 2). Other design needs included a frame to support the books and devices which would enable the monomer to be distributed to each book evenly. Allowances were also made for any changes in pressure during the processing, along with the ability to withstand a certain amount of rough handling.

The basic process steps are as follows:

(1) weigh and prepare books and secure in the frame. Place frame in container.
(2) seal the container and flush with nitrogen to remove residual oxygen from the container and within the paper fibre structure. (Oxygen is known to inhibit the polymerisation reaction.)
(3) introduce the monomer mixture under ambient conditions.

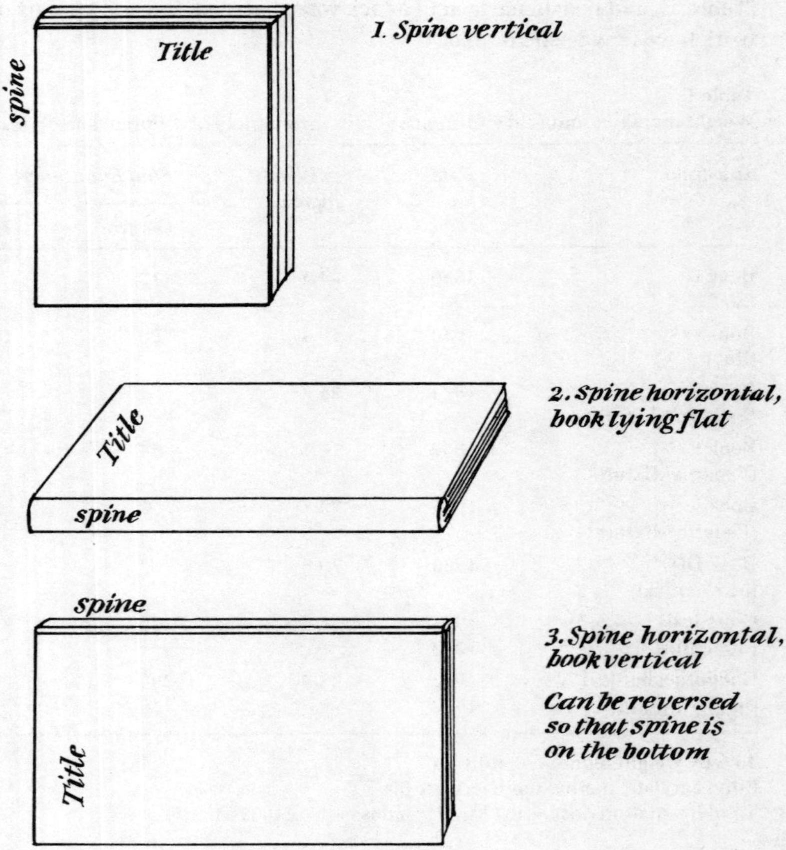

Figure 2

(4) equilibrate to allow an even distribution both within the books and between the books.

(5) initiate the polymerisation reaction by irradiating with gamma rays.

(6) remove any residual monomer/odour prior to returning the books for re-shelving.

The most important topics and hence those originally concentrated on were:

(a) methods of distributing the monomer to and within the books.

(b) assessing changes in temperature and pressure during irradiation.

(c) characterising the results of the polymerisation process on books.

(d) looking at various conservation treatments which may be applied to books which go through the polymerisation process.

Some of the early findings on the scale-up work were presented by Dr David Clements at the IADA Conference in Berlin, October 1987.[5]

Monomer distribution

It is important to achieve good monomer distribution in each page through a book, as well as between books. Ideally the equilibration period should be of minimum length to prevent risk of damage to inks, adhesives etc. The monomer is distributed by a combination of capillary transport and liquid/vapour phase diffusion. This process is akin to that of paper chromatography.

Various means of monomer transport into books were considered. These included drip feeding, spraying, injecting and wicking for liquid phase methods and also a vapour phase process. To date wicking and spraying/injecting are the methods which have been given most consideration; this has mainly been due to ease of operation for large scale processing.

Collection of data on temperature and pressure changes during processing

The use of thermocouples and differential pressure cells enables process changes during the irradiation stage to be recorded on a data logging system. Early results on this work showed that pressure changes were low and therefore future containers could be made out of light-weight materials. The temperature profiles showed a sharp rise as the reaction took off after an initial induction period. The temperature then rapidly dropped back to ambient. It is important to ensure that the temperature rise is well below that at which damage to the cellulose would occur. The aim is to keep temperature rises below 80°C. The radiation regime given to the containers is also important if consistent results are to be obtained. All the information being gained from this part of the experimental programme will help to optimise operating conditions on the main plant. It should also enable certain predictions to be made when conditions are changed.

Early pilot plant trials used a series of identical books, but more recent work has been done using mixed aged book samples (Tables 2 and 3). These are more representative of what will happen in the commercial plant. Books of different ages react at different times and rates and therefore in laying down a design brief, the operating cycles must cover all cases.

Characterisation of treated books

In general certain criteria need to be met from both the library's and plant operating points of view. Important criteria for the library are:

(a) to stop further degradation and preferably restore some of the lost strength.
(b) the life expectancy should be increased so that the books last for a further 50–100 years or longer.
(c) the dimensions of the book should not be altered significantly.
(d) the 'feel' of the paper should be similar.
(e) the treated books should not present any hazards to readers or library staff.
(f) the book should be receptive to other conservation treatments if possible.

Table 2
Pilot plant trials using five identical books to test consistency of results

Book no.	*Trial no.*	*% Weight increase*	*Relative % polymer yield on 20% target*
196B	7	18.8	94.0
197B	7	16.7	83.5
198B	7	17.5	87.5
199B	7	16.5	82.5
200B	7	18.9	94.5
		17.7	88.5 mean values
206B	9	18.2	91.0
207B	9	17.5	87.5
208B	9	19.3	96.5
209B	9	16.5	82.5
210B	9	17.2	86.0
		17.7	88.5

20% by weight monomer addition

Table 3
Pilot plant trials using a series of hardback aged books

Book no.	*Date*	*Trial no.*		*% Weight increase*
388B	1937	39		14.1
389B	1948	39		18.9
390B	—	39		17.3
391B	1954	39		20.5
			Mean	17.7
			S.D.	2.7
392B	1954	40		17.0
393B	1955	40		16.4
394B	1946	40		17.6
395B	1947	40		13.1
			Mean	16.1
			S.D.	2.0

25% by weight monomer addition

(g) the process should be suitable for a majority of books with the minimum of pre-sorting.
(h) the unit costs should be low.

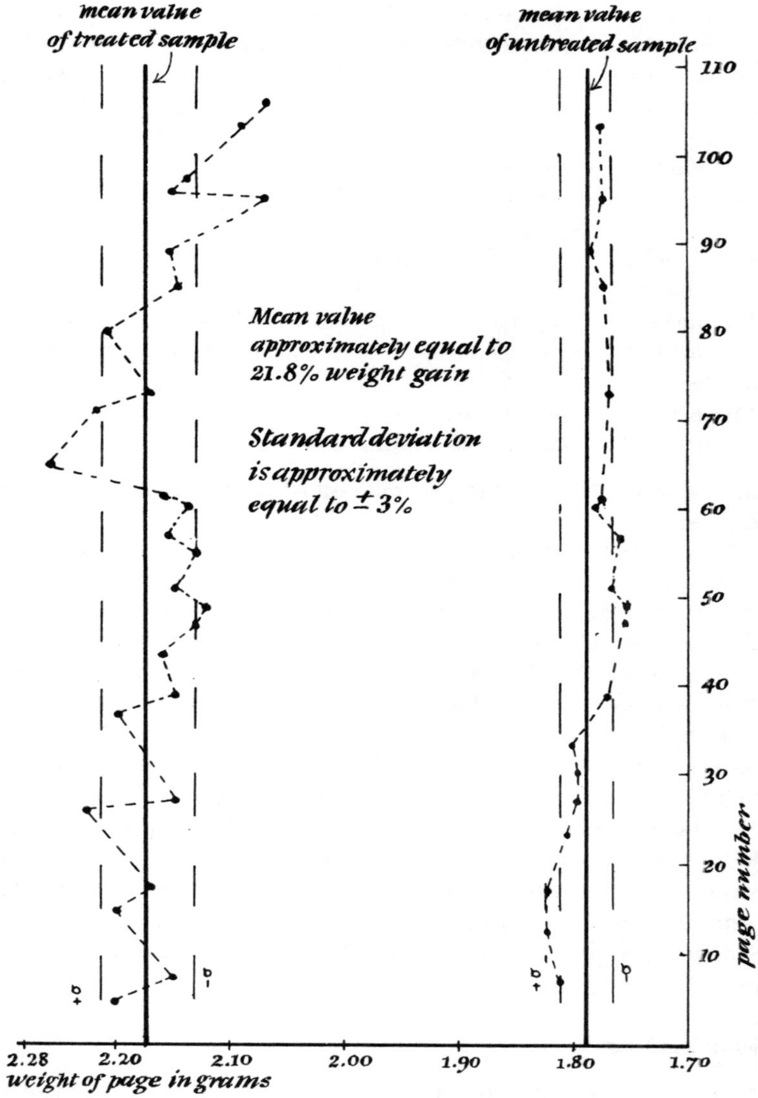

Figure 3: Mean weight gain from page to page throughout three identical books used in trial runs

Some of the conclusions from the trial work to date are as follows:

(1) good polymer yields can be achieved within the books.
(2) an even distribution of polymer between books is obtained.
(3) the page-to-page distribution is good provided sufficient time has been given during the equilibration period (Figure 3).
(4) residual monomer/odour can be removed by simple processing.

(5) good increases in strength are observed in most books, except those with fold values of less than 10; where more variable results occur.
(6) consistent results can be achieved between different trial runs using the same books.
(7) some modern dyes and toners can become mobile if very long equilibration times are given.
(8) the coloured plates tested to date show very little sign of change; as do printed photographs.
(9) older bindings are not usually affected by the process and only a few modern adhesives show slight change.
(10) the radiation regime must be constant in order to obtained consistent results for the whole range of books; hence a uniform irradiation path length is important.
(11) there is no residual radioactivity after treatment so the books can be handled as soon as processing is complete.

The above points are particularly relevant when considering the operation of the process.

Tests carried out on the treated samples include fold endurance, scanning electron microscopy (SEM), Fourier Transform Infra Red (FTIR) etc. SEM studies show that the polymer is distributed over the fibres and through the fibre network; the polymer is also deposited within the fibres. FTIR can be used to detect where the polymer has been deposited over a page, or to look at changes occuring to the cellulose or polymer during various testing work.

Most of the initial criteria set by the British Library have been met. However, one important point remains to be answered: how much longer will the treated books last compared to the untreated? Initial accelerated ageing studies gave encouraging results. Tests at 70°C and 50 per cent relative humidity over a ten day period showed that the fold values of untreated books fell by 50 per cent, while that of the treated books remained almost unchanged. More detailed ageing studies are now being carried out independently by the Paper Science Department at UMIST, Manchester and it is hoped to give further details in 1989.

Book handling

It is essential for consistent processing that all sections of every volume receive the same irradiation dose. The only way of achieving this is to ensure that the radiation path length through the books being treated is the same irrespective of the size and mass of the book collection. To achieve this end it is necessary to know the variation in the physical dimensions and masses of all books that are likely to be put through the process. Currently a group of people in the British Library are working on measuring randomly distributed clusters of books. When the data on book size and mass is complete it will be processed in order to define the mean book dimensions and the distribution of the British Library stock around these mean values. It is hoped to acquire data on some 20,000 books. This information is essential in order to develop packing and sorting procedures which will ensure a uniform irradiation path length for all possible mixtures of books in the treatment container.

Because of the complexities of sorting the books, one option may be to do this at the processing plant. Complete shelves of books would be sent down to the plant; here they would first be sorted; taking out books which are unsuitable for treatment. The rest of the books would then be arranged into size/weight groups ready for the first stage of the process. At the end of processing the treated and untreated books would be reunited prior to being returned to the library.

Although there are still issues to be resolved, especially with reference to scale-up problems, the general outlook is good. A feasibility study on a commercial plant with a throughput of 100,000–200,000 books per annum has been undertaken. These studies included the floor area requirements, chemical usage, safety factors and staffing levels etc. The detailed cost estimates suggest that the cost per book would be between £2–£4 depending upon throughput and capital repayment. However at present the market for bulk treatment processes has not been assessed.

The application of conservation techniques to treated paper

It is important to know what other conservation methods can be applied to paper which would be treated by the grafting technique. This is applicable to pre- and post conservation requirements. Some of this work has been undertaken independently by the Bodleian Library, Oxford and by the conservation workshops at the British Library. A set of identical books was used, half being treated by the grafting technique and the other half used as controls.

The tests carried out included:

(1) subjecting the sheets to washing and aqueous deacidification using magnesium bicarbonate. These gave pH values of 8.6 for treated and 8.7 for untreated sheets.
(2) spray deacidification with methyl magnesium carbonate.
(3) the use of traditional repair methods using Japanese tissue, with wheat and starch pastes.
(4) lamination with 10 gms tissue coated with Paraloid and Texicryl adhesives.
(5) subjecting deacidified and control samples to accelerated ageing tests.

Other testing work included removing the spine and rebinding the book using (i) PVA and (ii) animal glue. Additional lamination processes using Primal AC72 and removal of the lamination with industrial methylated spirits (IMS) were also carried out. All the test work gave very good results and suggests that many other conservation treatments could be applied.

Discussion

It is envisaged that within the next 18 months sufficient data should be available to confirm the feasibility of the process so that the bulk treatment of archival material at a rate of 200,000 volumes per annum will be possible, provided funds are forthcoming.

Notes

1. G M Cunha Mass deacidification for libraries *Library technology reports* May–June 1987 23(3) pp.361–472.
2. *Book preservation technologies* Congress of the United States Office of Technology Assessment. Washington DC 20510–8025; OTA–0–376 May 1988.
3. British Library *Treatment of archival material by graft polymerisation with monomer* UK Patent, GB 2,156,830 (24 February 1988).
4. British Library US Patent 4,724,158 (9 February 1988).
5. D W G Clements, C E Butler and C A Millington *Emerging technologies in paper strengthening: development and scale-up of graft copolymerisation technique,* Internationale Arbeitsgemein der Archiv, Bibliotheks-und Graphikrestauratoren, Conference. Berlin, October 1987.

Henry Heaney

Sharing information

Those who determined the title of this paper may not have realised that it can be interpreted in two ways – sharing information about what has been, is being, will be, should be preserved and sharing the information content of the publications themselves. I suspect that I am expected to deal with the former so I shall begin with the latter and I hope to show that the two should be related in our thinking.

If what concerns us and our readers is the information, or ideas, or thoughts contained in the items on our shelves, in most cases the format in which they are housed is less important than the content. The format is not unimportant. Printed books and journals are the norm because they have proved to be convenient. Nobody says: 'Bring back the clay tablets'. More modern media such as microfilm and microfiche are less convenient and less acceptable but the conservation needs of bindings and paper are so immense that we must have resort to them. The scale and extent of deterioration of paper-based stock render it uneconomic to plan for full-scale restoration of every copy of every book that has been affected.

The medium can in some cases, of course, form part or most of the message but this is true mainly for such subjects as historical bibliography or photographic history and I do not propose to be side-tracked into discussing the peculiar needs of those specialisms in this paper. I want first to consider microforms, produced either commercially or as a one-off, in-house. While we await a low-price, effective mass-deacidification process, microphotography is currently recognised as the cheapest way to produce satisfactory surrogates, however unattractive they may be to library users. Through the register of preservation microforms information is already being shared about material being preserved in this way. Microfilming, of course, has the added advantage that several copies can be produced from the master and placed in libraries which lacked a copy of the original or wished to withdraw it from regular use. Should some at least of library expenditure on commercially produced micro-reprints not be included as conservation commitment in financial returns such as the SCONUL survey reported upon at this seminar?

Another vehicle – electronic storage – also preserves data for posterity, though we are not yet quite sure how durable it is. It has, however, so many potential benefits that we must expect a technology to be perfected that will satisfy our doubts about its longevity. Electronic storage can be set up to allow wide dissemination, whether simply by viewing or after down-loading over a network. It has the added advantage that it can be searched and manipulated with greater dexterity and diversity than can any other medium. Indeed some data already exist only in electronic form, though archival policies for updated or superseded information still need to be worked out. I predict that if printed journal prices continue to rise as meteorically as they have risen for several years now, there will soon be greater recourse to electronic publishing, with on-demand print out, as the only way off the rocket which has been accelerating not only on the initiative of rapacious publishers, whom libraries seem powerless to resist, but also by current pressures on researchers to publish more if they want to be promoted. On-demand printing has another side-effect which accords with currently fashionable thinking on the relevance and impact of research. Tallies of what has been off-printed or downloaded could be readily obtained and, alongside the dubiously valid citation data, would attract our financial masters as seeming to show the usefulness of what has been revealed, and therefore the effectiveness of their investment in its discovery.

We are all familiar with bibliographic and factual information databases but there are also some full-text databases created for scholarly research. ARTFL, the American and French Research Treasury of the French Language, is an interesting example. It holds some 1,500 French language texts from the 18th century onwards. The idea arose out of the French government's desire in 1957 to create a new dictionary. The texts were needed as a word-bank to support the project but they are now important in their own right. Since 1984, ARTFL has been available for on-line searching using the Oxford Concordance Package and is to be developed as a central depository of French literature, history and political science for the scholarly community. A similar project could be set up for British studies. There would be problems of capital investment, maintenance cost, access charges, and user-friendliness but against the unthinkable costs of individual libraries preserving individual volumes, a central programme of this kind would clearly be more economic, more innovative and more likely to attract funding. British chauvenism will also be stimulated by the Franco-American lead. There will be difficulties, of course, in determining priorities for what is to be mounted and in what order but these are rather like those at present faced by reprint publishers and, if nationally directed, with backing from scholarly bodies such as the British Academy and professional groupings, including librarians, they could be effectively addressed. Is this, I ask you, not a more imaginative use of limited resources in a technological age than the haphazard piecemeal approach which we have envisaged individually or sectionally hitherto?

Some librarians among us will naturally be concerned about the need in all of this for bibliographic control. If data have been converted into machine-readable form in a network-orientated environment, potential users need to be made aware of what is available. Logically this information ought to be stored alongside the mainstream bibliographical databases which are now emerging in Britain and will soon become routine apparatus for the literature-searching element in research. I do not deny the need for intensive wooing to make such a marriage.

I do some literature searching myself and ARTFL came to my attention in a report on some of the proceedings of the 1987 annual meeting of the Modern Language Association in San Francisco.[1] The title of that report, *Online databases and book preservation,* seemed so germane for me in preparing this paper that I sought it with alacrity. The author, however, had merely singled out a few of the 721 sessions at San Francisco which might particularly interest librarians. One, on ARTFL, she had herself chaired. Another presented an overview of current and future developments in online literary databases and advocated the publication, presumably in hard copy, of a directory of them, so numerous are they. Partnerships among kindred database providers are, apparently, beginning to be forged. Interestingly enough Cambridge University was cited as one of the institutions with which the MLA is negotiating.

The third session described in some detail activities to cope with the preservation crisis in United States libraries. One of the speakers, John Haeger, who is a senior officer in the Research Libraries Group, is quoted as saying 'the only viable solution to the preservation of books is microfilming'. He recognised that, even in the United States, this is still at a cottage-industry level and he, with other speakers, went on to discuss various options for coordination.

Now the remarkable thing is not that the title of the article was misleading and promised too much but that there had been no insight in the discussions at the MLA that preservation needs and on-line opportunities should be correlated. Perhaps MLA is the wrong forum, too large, too diffuse, for such ideas to be aired until they have matured a little more. Perhaps they find their birth in gatherings such as this, specialising in preservation but drawing upon expertise and information on trends in other fields.

In this regard, one development is particularly timely. In Britain we have the beginnings of a quasi-national bibliographic database, bringing together the bibliographic records of the seven large academic libraries who are members of CURL, the Consortium of University Research Libraries: Cambridge, Edinburgh, Glasgow, Leeds, London (Senate House), Manchester and Oxford (Bodleian). Using software devised in Cambridge University Library, the entire bibliographic records of the big seven's catalogues in so far as they are in machine-readable form are now being mounted at Manchester on a machine supported by the Computer Board as a national facility. The records will be searched from a central index, making it unnecessary to merge the individual libraries' files. This venture has been launched with funds released by the University Grants Committee and should in eighteen months time be widely available for access by all institutions connected to the Joint Academic Network over the JANET link. At present JANET is open to all universities and polytechnics engaged in research. The British Library is also connected and the National Libraries of Scotland and Wales will be linked in the coming months.

It is not appropriate here to expatiate upon the immense potential which the CURL database will offer for closer cooperation among its member libraries and throughout JANET. In the present context we should note that the database will provide a vehicle to record and announce the preservation status of individual items noted there. No steps have been taken so far to add any information of this kind but the Research Libraries Group on their RLIN database have shown what can be achieved.[2] The USMARC structure has field 007 which can be used for the physical description of items. It does not feature in UKMARC but could be released for this purpose. RLIN notes in 007 the physical format of a microform (film, fiche etc) and the generation (preservation master, printing master or first generation). Further refinement, using a different field unique to RLIN, enables preservation intentions to be recorded and searched. From the QD (queuing date) field a member library will discover if another already intends to microfilm a title and how this is likely to be done, thus encouraging collaboration and streamlining effort.

In the same article, Kruger notes the conversion to machine-readable format of the National Register of Microfilm Masters in the United States and collaboration by ten RLG members on microfilming monographs published between 1870 and 1920 in certain Library of Congress classification classes. Periodicals will follow. RLIN users can identify what has been done and what is in the pipeline directly on the network. Other libraries can subscribe to a fiche printout of the information. On this side of the Atlantic we should not duplicate work already done or being done in the United States. We need first to know what has been microfilmed or captured electronically there. We must also coordinate programmes to avoid unnecessary future duplication.

The Research Libraries Group has examined the problem of adding a description of the physical condition of items on the RLIN database to the records. A comprehensive six-scale code for paper and another for binding, drawn up by John Dean and John Baker, has proved too daunting for full implementation but now seems to have value as a local input option to help determine local priorities. But even these are of wider significance. If UKMARC fields can be released to indicate the physical condition of an item, even without a national programme there is value in knowing that a certain library has already microfilmed or deacidified or copied an item on to acid-free paper. RLG and OCLC regularly exchange title-related information on their members' holdings of master microfilms; the quasi-national database that is emerging in Britain could likewise be extended to hold supplementary preservation details, including future plans, not necessarily confined to the contributing participants.

Let us suppose that we can add MARC format preservation statements to a quasi-national database and that other libraries adopt the same fields. For discussion purposes at least, let us also accept that preservation as well as being by boxing or repair or rebinding or microfilming or deacidification may also be by conversion into machine-readable forms. We need then to take merely a baby step to add a reference to the full-text data in the bibliographic database, indicating whether it is held at a national centre or in a local machine. Obviously only if the text can be accessed would such information be helpful.

To achieve this breakthrough, conservators and librarians and archivists will need the strong backing of the potential users, the scholars and researchers. Commercial vendors will probably also become interested and it is a truism that in the present political climate the early involvement of the private sector would be essential to the success of the enterprise. Dearth of such partnership has limited the progress that we have made in preservation hitherto. This widening of interest will be essential also in determining priorities but experience to date is not encouraging.

Left to themselves, librarians can doubtless devise many sensible schemes for selecting what to preserve. The more enlightened of us would probably build upon the Conspectus technique, an RLG-devised methodology touched upon by Bernard Naylor[3] at last year's Seminar to evaluate the varying strengths of library collections in different subjects. This leads, *inter alia,* to the acceptance of prime collecting responsibilities for a particular topic by individual libraries on behalf of the others. It would be natural for this to extend to prime preservation responsibilities for that range of material as well. But such an approach, by its very nature will not cover every subject. Haeger at San Francisco described another policy, which he called the vacuum cleaner approach, whereby an RLG member chooses a field within later 19th to early 20th century publishing (the period of greatest deterioration) and microfilms all its brittle books classified within that field. The flaw is that every title is an equal candidate with every other. Why not ask the users to identify the more important titles? If a project conducted by the American Philological Association is any guide, this policy can be just as ineffective. Scholars disagree in identifying key titles; committees consume time and time is what we have not got. As an aside, I would say that, though not directly related to preservation needs, the commercially-floated nineteenth century text microfiche programme in this country is equally unpromising. Academics and librarians advise, the publisher exercises commercial acumen but the lists and the order in which they are appearing puzzle me for one.

Another approach, for which, with the CURL database, we are putting the mechanism in place, is that we should concentrate on works in the major libraries. Academic libraries' stock will, of course, reflect the demands of the curriculum and research intensity at the time of publication. These change over the years and may well, even across the big seven, under-represent areas of study which are of current interest or of potential future interest. I wish I could be as confident as Ogden, head of the preservation programme at Berkeley, who is reported to have said at San Francisco that scholars can spot new trends and alert their libraries. The strength of the CURL libraries, however, is that they include two of the current legal deposit libraries and two others which had legal deposit privileges until 1836. Moreover, they all hold special collections with nineteenth and twentieth century stock, given or bequeathed by booklovers with broader collecting interests than that of the university itself. Preservation policy must, however, extend beyond the holdings of the national and major academic libraries; nevertheless it must follow a planned programme in determining priorities.

Too much concentration on such problems distracts from the vision of opportunity that networking will bring. It is time to draw the strands together. Allied to preservation through traditional methods and microreproduction we must also now acknowledge the electronic record, with its unique facility for flexible searching. Computers can assist in the bibliographical recording of preservation activity, aided by an opening up of UKMARC to give copy form and physical condition. A quasi-national database for the catalogues of the seven major university research libraries is in the offing and will be accessible over the joint academic network, to which the catalogues of the three national libraries will also be linked. Researchers already use JANET for other forms of data communication and access to non-library databases. Text databases already exist and more are being developed. A British equivalent to ARTFL would bring preservation benefits, especially if it could be accessed via JANET. There is room for scholars, researchers, librarians and the commercial sector to collaborate. Firm and positive decisions on a planned, prioritised programme for preservation electronically will be difficult to reach. The costs will still be prodigious but there is this consolation: if we make mistakes in selecting texts for electronic conversion which later prove to be in low demand the conversion and dissemination costs will have been no greater than those of the alternatives open to us. Moreover, since publishers increasingly hold their texts on magnetic tape for reprinting or revision in a new edition should they not be required under copyright law to deposit copies of the tapes for archival purposes as well, or in one copy at least, instead of the printed text? But if we decide to take this path, much lobbying and persuasion will be needed to get it tarmacadamed. We can, however, learn through lobbies:

Waiting for a visiting friend in the lobby of a Glasgow hotel recently, I overheard another visitor being met by a local Glaswegian. The visitor had a question and a comment. 'Do you have a good bookshop here, with staff who know what books they have? Because librarians don't know any more – they're all computerised.'

Notes

1. D Mihram *Online databases and book preservation.* In: *C&RL news* March 1988.
2. B Kruger *Automating preservation information in RLIN.* In: *Library resources and technical services* vol.32 April 1988.
3. B Naylor *Conservation and Conspectus.* In: *Conservation and collection management* London: British Library, 1988 ISBN 0 7123 0149 6 (Proceedings of the 1987 National Preservation Office seminar).